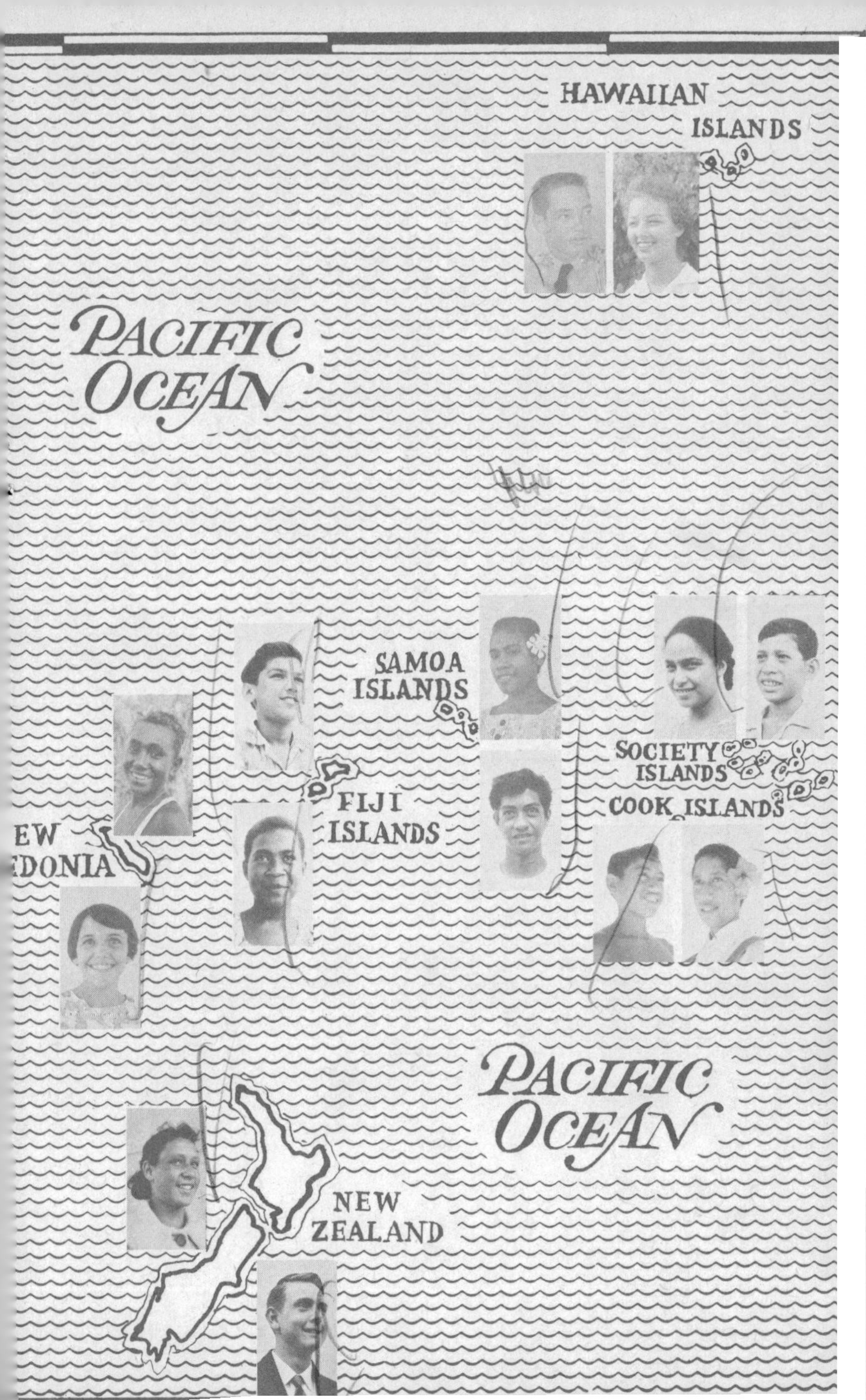
HAWAIIAN
ISLANDS
PACIFIC
OCEAN
SAMOA
ISLANDS
FIJI
ISLANDS
SOCIETY
ISLANDS
COOK ISLANDS
EW
DONIA
PACIFIC
OCEAN
NEW
ZEALAND

Young People
of
the Pacific Islands

BOOKS BY CHARLES R. JOY

Young People of the Eastern Mediterranean
Young People of the Western Mediterranean
Young People of East Asia and Australia
Young People of West Africa
Young People of East and South Africa
Young People of Mexico and Central America
Young People of South America
Young People of the Pacific Islands
Africa. A Handbook for Travelers
Emerging Africa. A Scholastic World Affairs Multi-Text
Light in the Dark Continent: People of the African Equator
Island in the Desert: Challenge of the Nile Valley
Desert Caravans: Challenge of the Changing Sahara
Food and Population: Challenge of a Hungry World
Getting to Know Israel
Getting to Know the Two Chinas
Getting to Know the South Pacific
Getting to Know Hong Kong
Getting to Know Tanganyika
Getting to Know the Amazon
Getting to Know the Sahara
Getting to Know El Salvador, Nicaragua, and Costa Rica
The Africa of Albert Schweitzer (co-author)
The Animal World of Albert Schweitzer
Music in the Life of Albert Schweitzer
Wit and Wisdom of Albert Schweitzer

EDITED BY CHARLES R. JOY

Harper's Topical Concordance
Lyof Tolstoy, An Anthology
Albert Schweitzer, An Anthology

TRANSLATED BY CHARLES R. JOY

A Psychiatric Study of Jesus, by Albert Schweitzer
Goethe, by Albert Schweitzer

Young People of the Pacific Islands

THEIR STORIES IN THEIR OWN WORDS

by
CHARLES R. JOY

DUELL, SLOAN AND PEARCE
New York

First Edition

Grateful acknowledgment is made to **Junior Scholastic**, the magazine in which some of these stories have been published in a different and briefer form. Other stories appear here for the first time.

Library of Congress Catalogue Card Number: 63-10362

Manufactured in the United States of America for Meredith Press

Affiliate of
MEREDITH PRESS
Des Moines & New York

CONTENTS

Note: The islands of Japan, Taiwan, Hong Kong, the Philippines, and Indonesia are included in *Young People of East Asia and Australia.*

FOREWORD

It was John Quincy Adams, our sixth president, who said a hundred and sixty years ago, "Westward the star of empire takes its way." He was delivering an oration at Plymouth, and of course, he was thinking of the *Mayflower*, which sailed westward to the shores of New England to form a new nation there.

Ever since that day the great movements of our history have been westward. The pioneers pushed westward across the prairies and the mountains until they reached the Pacific. The explorers, the adventurers, the missionaries, the traders sailed westward to the romantic lands of the South Seas. The Second World War carried multitudes of our men to the rim of Asia. The star of our fiftieth state rises from the western waves.

Horace Greeley, one of our greatest newspaper editors, once gave some sound advice to aspiring young men. He said: "The best business you can go into you will find on your father's farm or in his workshop. If you have no family or friends to aid you, and no prospects opened to you there, turn your face to the great West, and there build up a home and fortune."

In this, the eighth book of our Young People's series, we turn our face to the scattered isles of the Pacific. The young men whom Horace Greeley was addressing will find, if they travel to this far west, young people like themselves, who are dreaming of a better future.

Many of us have learned about these distant places from such books as *Robinson Crusoe*, *Moby Dick*, *Mutiny on the*

Bounty. On the whole these books give a very imperfect picture of these far-off places.

It is the author's hope that the present book will give you a glimpse of young people on these islands who, like you, want to build a home and a fortune. Here they are waiting to greet you in all friendliness: Polynesians, Melanesians, Micronesians, and others. They call themselves Hawaiians, Cook Islanders, Tahitians, Fijians, Maoris, French, and Japanese. But they are not so different after all from you. You will enlarge your vision and enrich your life as you come to know them.

Here are real boys and girls, who tell you their stories in their own words.

Young People
of
the Pacific Islands

1. THE PACIFIC ISLANDS

UNDERSTANDING THE PACIFIC OCEAN

To get a true picture of the Pacific Ocean many of us will have to begin by forgetting almost everything we've heard about it. In the first place, it's not just another ocean. It's the greatest of them all. It's twenty times as big as the United States. As a matter of fact, it's bigger than all the land in the world. If you could fit the continents and islands neatly together, every one of them, and drop this enormous piece of real estate into the Pacific, there'd still be some hundreds of miles of open sea all around the edges. From Panama to the western shore of the China Sea the distance is about eleven thousand miles.

ISLANDS AND EMPTY PLACES

Of course, it isn't all water. There are many islands in it. So many that no one has ever counted them. You'd have to guess the number, and no matter how many you dared to guess, you'd probably be wrong. For there are hundreds of thousands of islands in this ocean. Many of them have no name.

Does that mean you find islands everywhere you go? Not at all. The Pacific in general is a very empty, a very lonely place. If you should draw a tiny picture of a coral island, just big enough to hold a single coconut tree and yourself, on a huge sheet of otherwise blank paper, it would give you a fairly good idea of what the Pacific is like in most places.

Ferdinand Magellan was the first man to sail across it. He traveled for ninety-two days and all he saw was two wee islands where no one lived. Another great explorer, Captain James Cook, once sailed on it for ten thousand miles, and never saw any land at all. Most of the islands we are going to visit are in the western and southern part of the Pacific. But even there you find enormous empty spaces.

THE PACIFIC DEEPS

The Pacific is not only the biggest of all the oceans. It's the deepest too. The average depth of this sea is almost three miles. But there are holes in it much deeper than that. These holes are called deeps whenever the bottom lies more than 18,000 feet below the surface. There are thirty-three of these deeps in the Pacific. By contrast the Indian Ocean has only five. The deepest known spot in all the oceans is south of the Mariana Islands. This is the Mariana Trench. It's 35,640 feet deep! Suppose you could drop Mount Everest, which is 29,141 feet high, into the bottom of this hole, and then pile Mount Washington, which is 6,288 feet high, on top of it. Any vessel sailing over the Tiptop House on Mount Washington would still have several hundreds of feet of water beneath its keel.

You can see from this that the bottom of the Pacific is far from being a flat plain. There are plateaus and valleys and mountains, volcanoes and coral islands and reefs far below the surface of the sea.

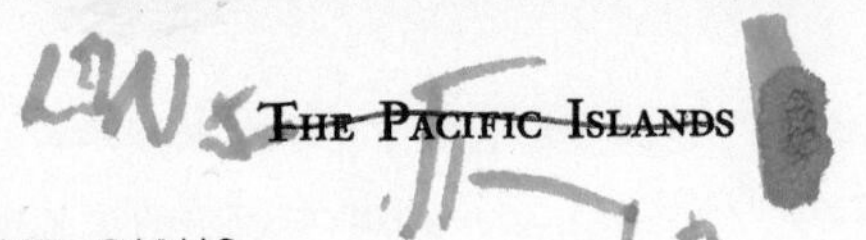

STORMS AND CALMS

When Magellan had passed around the southern tip of South America, the great ocean which he entered was so quiet compared with the frightful storms he had just encountered that he called it the Pacific. During the next few months there were long periods when he prayed for the slightest gust of wind to ruffle the surface of the sea, and to fill his slack sails. Recently a small tug towed two liberty ships all the way across the ocean from Panama to Japan. The trip was a monotonous journey of sixty-seven days, all of them exactly alike: cloudless skies, calm seas, oppressive heat. There are Pacific sailors who have never seen anything but moderate seas and winds.

This is not always true, however. When a little later we visit some of the islands in the western Pacific, we shall hear about violent storms called typhoons. There are almost 150 of these frightful hurricanes every year in this part of the world, and waves have been recorded more than 110 feet high.

Still most of these typhoons whirl around harmlessly in the open sea and do no damage at all.

You can call the Pacific a stormy sea or a placid one. It depends a good deal on your luck and your location.

OCEANIA

Nowhere else in the world are there so many important island groups as you find in the Pacific. All of them together are often called Oceania. This term does not include the Aleutian Islands, which swing westward in a long arc from Alaska to the Kamchatka Peninsula of the Soviet Union, and separate the North Pacific from the Bering Sea. It does not include the islands along the American coast or, at least in this book, the islands of Indonesia. It does not include Australia, which belongs to Asia because of its fauna and flora. But it does include New Zealand, because the animals and plants found there are those of Oceania.

POLYNESIA

The island groups themselves are found scattered in three great areas. The best-known of these is Polynesia. If you draw a big triangle on the map to include the Hawaiian Islands in the north, Easter Island far to the southeast and New Zealand far to the southwest you will have the area occupied by the Polynesian islands. Each leg of that triangle is from 4,500 to 4,800 miles long.

Easter Island is just a lonely rock which was discovered on Easter Sunday in 1722 by a Dutch captain. It has some very strange, stern-looking statues of great size on it, some of them weighing as much as fifty tons. Once the island had a population of about 6,000, but now there are only about 250 people left. The other points of this great triangle, Hawaii and New Zealand, we shall visit later in this book.

The word Polynesia comes from two Greek words. *Nesos* means "island"; *polus* means "many." So this is the place of the many islands. They are lovely islands, most of them. The Hawaiians call their archipelago the Paradise of the Pacific. Some of the Society Islands have been called the most beautiful islands in the world. There is an old legend that the Garden of Eden was really in Samoa. People thought so, because it was so wonderfully attractive.

MELANESIA

West of Polynesia lie two other large island areas. In the south is the region called Melanesia. The Greek word *melas* means "black," so this is the place of the black islands. They are so called because the people who settled there had dark skins, thick black beards, and black frizzy hair.

MICRONESIA

North of Melanesia is another huge area dotted with many small islands. This is Micronesia. *Mikros* is Greek for "small." There are in this part of the Pacific thousands of tiny islands, settled by people who are not as dark as the Melanesians and not as light as the Polynesians.

THE EQUATOR

The actual location of Melanesia and Micronesia in the Pacific can best be given by reference to two imaginary lines that run through the ocean.

We all know of the equator, the imaginary line that runs east and west around the middle of the earth to separate the Southern Hemisphere from the Northern. Ships that cross this line always have an amusing ceremony at this point in their voyage. Father Neptune, the god of the sea, comes on board with a long beard and a grass costume. He carries a trident, or a spear with three prongs. He is accompanied by a queer crew dressed in more strange costumes. All the polliwogs (they are the passengers who have never crossed the equator before) are asked to come forward. Each of them has to do a stunt, sing a song, recite a poem, stand on his head, and so on. You won't forget your initiation if you have once crossed the equator.

THE INTERNATIONAL DATE LINE

There is another imaginary line that is much more difficult to explain. It's the international date line, and it cuts the Pacific Ocean in two from north to south. Almost all the way it follows the 180th meridian. A meridian is a half circle that extends from pole to pole. You'll find the 180th meridian marked on the map as 180°. To number the meridians you start from Greenwich, England. Greenwich is 0°, and halfway round the earth, going either east or west, we reach the 180th meridian.

The earth turns towards the east, towards the sunrise. It turns around once every twenty-four hours. So the sun seems to be moving towards the west every day. People have agreed that when they cross the date line from the east they will lose a day, and Monday will suddenly become Tuesday. Traveling in the opposite direction they will gain a day and have two Mondays instead of one.

For the most part the international date line passes only over the ocean, but it does cross a few small islands. In these places you sometimes have funny situations. A woman stands in the door of her hut on a Monday morning and calls to her boy who is fishing on the shore. But it's Tuesday morning for the boy. When he comes back with the fish he has caught, it will take him a whole day to walk from the shore to his hut though it's only a hundred yards away, and he'll be walking backwards from Tuesday to Monday.

You'd think that these people would get very confused over the date line, but they don't bother about it at all. The boy has caught the fish that his mother will boil in a pot over the fire. That for the moment is all that matters for either of them.

LOCATING THE ISLANDS

Now the islands east of the date line are in Polynesia. New Zealand is, too, though it's west of the date line. The islands west of the date line and south of the equator, with the exception of New Zealand, are in Melanesia. The islands west of the date line and north of the equator are mostly in Micronesia.

THE EARLY NAVIGATORS

How did these early navigators sail over the vast empty spaces of the Pacific and reach the islands where they settled?

They had no compass or other instrument of navigation. Still we know from our study of history that lack of such instruments never stopped the adventurers. The Vikings crossed the Atlantic in their "long ships" with the high prows and sterns and square sails. They had no sextants. The Arabs sailed over the Indian Ocean in their dhows for many centuries before the compass was known. Their lateen sails became as much a symbol of the Moslem faith as the crescent, and they were seen in all the important ports in East Africa and South Asia.

The Polynesians had no instruments, but they had the stars, the clouds, the ocean currents, the winds, and the birds to guide them.

They knew the Pole Star of the northern skies and the Southern Cross of the southern skies. The latter has four stars that look like a square. Close by is the False Cross with four stars and an extra one in the center. There is no southern pole star but south of the Southern Cross there is a black space in the Milky Way. It's called the Coal Sack, and the Coal Sack marks the South Pole.

These early sailors watched the clouds also. The clouds showed how the winds were blowing. Often they hovered around the top of a mountain, and in the distance might be a sign of land.

They knew the ocean currents. Some of these currents are so huge that they are called drifts, not currents. They are really mighty rivers in the sea. There is a North Equatorial Current that flows to the west just above the equator. There's a South Equatorial Current that flows in the same direction just below the equator. Between them is an Equatorial Countercurrent that flows east.

The North Pacific Drift is a massive current that flows clockwise in the North Pacific. In the west it turns north, meets the colder waters there, and then turns south along the western shore of North America. A similar drift in the South

Pacific runs counterclockwise and flows up along the western shore of South America, where it is known as the Peru Current. In time these early navigators learned about these ocean rivers and took advantage of them.

But sometimes they wanted to move against the current. Then they found the winds might help them. Most important were the trade winds. They were the cold winds that blew towards the equator from the north and the south. In the Northern Hemisphere they came from the northeast, in the Southern Hemisphere from the southeast. They didn't blow straight south or north, because of the motion of the earth eastward. The word trade here has nothing to do with a vocation. It means a customary course or direction.

When the trades approach the equator they begin to rise with the heat. So there are hardly any winds there at all. Instead there's a belt of sea about six hundred miles wide that is called the doldrums. This was a bad place for the old sailing vessels. Sometimes there were violent squalls but more often the sea was like a hot, shining mirror without a breath of wind for weeks at a time. This was torture for the sailing ships, but the men of the early dugouts had paddles.

North and south of the trades are the Horse Latitudes, a region where ships were becalmed again, and the horses on board died or were thrown overboard to lighten the vessel.

The birds helped to guide these early navigators also. The birds, as we all know, fly regular routes in their great migrations. Usually they nest on land every night. There are legends that the early Polynesians were guided to Hawaii by the golden plover, and that the shining cuckoo led another fleet of canoes from the Solomon Islands to New Zealand.

It was by these means that the early adventurers found the new homes they were looking for. They set out in the dugouts they had hewn from great logs. A big platform was built over a pair of these boats and a great sail rigged in the bow. The paddlers sat in the dugouts on either side. On the platform a shelter rose, in which the women and children slept. The women cooked on a table of sand surrounded by rocks on the deck of their ship. They had a cargo of pigs and hens and dogs, of seed plants to be set out in their new home, of food, and tools, and other supplies for the voyage and the new settlement.

So equipped and so guided they traveled from places like New Guinea to places like Easter Island, eight thousand miles away to the southeast. Such voyages remain a marvel in the story of the sea.

In this chapter we have given the briefest kind of introduction to the mighty Pacific, its islands, and its people. We shall learn much more about it as we visit the boys and girls who live there.

2. HAWAII

OUR FIFTIETH STAR

THE GIRDLE OF FIRE

In all the world there are about five hundred active volcanoes besides thousands of inactive ones. Some three hundred of the active volcanoes rise like flaming torches around the shores of the Pacific. Only one of these is in the continental United States, Lassen Peak in California. But up in Alaska and in the Aleutian Islands there are several more. When you take a Northwest Airlines flight to Japan you can see them smoking along the horizon.

In this whole great ocean area there have been 1,974 eruptions from 1800 to 1914. And this doesn't count the El Salvador volcano Izalco, called the Lighthouse of the Pacific, which was erupting about every ten minutes during the whole of this period.

Some of these Pacific eruptions have been spectacular. The great volcano Krakatau in Indonesia blew off its top in the frightful explosion of 1883. The ashes spread around the world.

THE GIFT OF THE VOLCANOES

The Hawaiian Islands are of volcanic origin. Thousands of years ago some of the undersea volcanoes (there are still thirty-four known active ones there) began to erupt. The lava that came up from holes in the ocean floor hardened in little cones. More eruptions followed and the cones grew higher and higher until the tops of them appeared above the surface of the sea. The lava crumbled and became soil. The rains made streams and valleys. The birds brought seeds. The lovely Hawaiian Islands began to take shape.

Mauna Loa (the word means the "long mountain") on the biggest of the islands, which is called Hawaii, is the largest active volcano in the world today. It's 13,680 feet high. Its rivers of lava in some places flowed right to the sea and became hard as stone. The old legend said that this volcano was the home of Pele, the fire goddess. It still erupts every few years. That means that Pele is *huhu*, or "angry."

Mount Kilauea is thought to be just another outlet for Mauna Loa, and it's very active. In 1959 it "blew its lid" and the molten lava destroyed hundreds of acres of farms and orchards. On the edge of the crater there is a hotel that heats its rooms with steam from the volcano. You can see the flowing lava and the fountain of fire without danger. Mauna Loa and Kilauea are what the geologists call "quiet" volcanoes. The lava is so hot and so liquid that it's never hurled into the air in terrific explosions. It just runs over the rim of the crater and flows down the side.

Mauna Kea (the "white mountain") is capped with snow and is inactive. It's the highest mountain in the Pacific, 13,784 feet high. But its base lies far below the level of the sea, so that it's actually 31, 750 feet high. That makes it the highest mountain in the world, for Mount Everest, as we have already learned, is only 29,141 feet high.

On another of the Hawaiian Islands, Maui, there is a ten-thousand-foot sleeping volcano, Mount Haleakala. Its crater is called the House of the Sun, and it's twenty miles around the rim of it. You could drop all of New York City into it. From the crater, if you are lucky, you can see your own shadow on a lower cloud with a rainbow around it.

If Egypt is the gift of the Nile, Hawaii is the gift of the volcano.

THE FLEET OF ISLANDS

Mark Twain said that Hawaii was "the loveliest fleet of islands anchored in any sea." Of course, you couldn't persuade the people of Tahiti or Mooréa or New Zealand that this is true, but you can understand why the Hawaiians say *Hawaii no ka oy*, which means "There's no place like Hawaii."

These islands are the loneliest group in the whole Pacific. They are 2,100 miles from San Francisco, 2,100 from the Aleutians, 3,400 from Tokyo, 4,400 from Sydney, almost 4,700 from Panama, and 4,800 from Manila.

The islands form a long chain running for over 1,600 miles from southeast to northwest. Eight of them in the southeast are inhabited. But there are many little unpeopled islands up in the northwest. The inhabited islands occupy 375 miles of the chain, and they have a delightful semitropical climate. About half a million people live in them. The largest island is the one with the volcanoes we have been talking about. This is the island of Hawaii. The people call it the Big Island. It's famous for its orchids as well as its volcanoes, its black sand beaches, and its memories of Captain Cook, who discovered the islands.

The most important island is Oahu, because that's where the capital, Honolulu, is located. The city has about 250,000 people in it. Just above it is the crater of another of Hawaii's many volcanoes. This one is extinct, and in the crater, which is called the Punch Bowl, is a national cemetery. It was from this crater that lava once flowed down into the sea to form the land on which the city of Honolulu now stands. Nearby is the great Pearl Harbor Naval Base, the scene of the 1941 surprise attack by the Japanese. The city has more than sixty hotels, wonderful beaches such as Waikiki's "Mile of Romance," lovely residences, and important business houses.

The island itself is made up of two mountain ranges, and most of the people live between the mountains and the sea. In giving directions they say *mauka*, which means "toward the mountains," and *makai*, which means "toward the sea."

For the tourist this is *Aloha* Land. The word means all kinds of lovely things: "welcome, farewell, our love to you, come back soon." *Aloha* Land is the land of surf-riding, of sunbathing, of outrigger canoes, of catamarans (sailboats with two hulls), of hula dances, and ukuleles, of *luaus* (a "feast" of roast pork cooked in a hole in the ground filled with hot stones), and of many other delightful things.

Maui is the Valley Island, and here at Lahaina was the old capital of the Hawaiian kings.

Lanai is the Pineapple Island. It's just one big pineapple plantation. Sometimes 400,000 pineapples are shipped out in a single day.

Molokai is nearest to Oahu, and is famous as the place where a colony of those who suffered from Hansen's disease (often called leprosy) was established. Here Father Damien, the devoted Belgian priest, ministered to those unfortunate outcasts until he himself contracted the disease and died.

Northwest of Oahu is the exquisitely beautiful Kauai, called the Garden Island. It's one of the wettest spots on earth, with an annual rainfall of 471 inches. That's why the flowers are so wonderful there.

THE SANDWICH ISLANDS

The early Polynesians came from somewhere in the west Pacific. Their primitive ships sailed down to the Samoa Islands, the Cook Islands, and the Society Islands. A second migration brought them from these places to the Hawaiian Islands about a thousand years ago. As we have seen, they took along with them not only their families but also food, plants, and animals.

Many years passed before Captain James Cook, one of the greatest of all the English explorers, discovered the people living there. This was in 1778. He had a good friend in England and he named the islands for him. He was the Earl of Sandwich, and for many years the islands were called the Sandwich Islands. The islanders at first thought Captain Cook was one of their own gods, who had left them years before promising to return. They could not do enough for him. But when he came back a year later trouble arose between the natives and the sailors. The people began to realize that Cook was not a god at all and they killed him.

Captain Cook was the Columbus of the Pacific.

Soon after the natives of the Hawaiian Islands were unified under a single king, whose name was Kamehameha. He was the George Washington of the islands. He died in 1819 but the monarchy continued until 1893, when Queen Liliuokalani was dethroned and a republic proclaimed. On July 7, 1898, Hawaii was annexed by the United States, and on March 12, 1959, the United States made Hawaii our fiftieth state.

THE HAWAIIAN MIXING BOWL

The early Polynesians found life very easy when they had once established themselves on their islands. They lived on fruit and roots and fish and there were plenty of these all around them. The people led a gay, happy, carefree life.

Then missionaries came from Boston to teach them that the old gods were false gods and to win them to a new way of life. The descendants of the missionaries began to grow sugar cane and pineapples in huge plantations. They needed men to work in the fields and in the canneries. But the Polynesians had enough to eat and they did not like that kind of work. So the owners of the big plantations had to go abroad to bring in workers. They brought in Japanese, Filipinos, Chinese, and other peoples. Today, because these people intermarried, there are very few pure Hawaiians left. Maybe there are only about twenty thousand of them. But these many different peoples live very happily together. It's a lesson for all mankind in these troubled days.

THE HAWAIIAN LANGUAGE

This is a Polynesian language, of course, and Polynesian is spoken all through the great triangle we have drawn on the map and in New Zealand also.

The alphabet is very simple, just twelve letters. There are five vowels, *a*, *e*, *i*, *o*, *u*, pronounced *ah*, *ay*, *ee*, *oh*, *oo*, and seven consonants, *h*, *k*, *l*, *m*, *n*, *p*, and *w*, all with the English sounds. Every vowel is pronounced, no matter how many of them come together. *Kamaaina* means "born on the islands." It's pronounced *kah-mah-ah-ee-nah*. In the beginning the Polynesians had no written language.

Our Hawaiian girl, Indira Karma Hale, is of mixed blood, like many others. She lives on the lovely Kona Coast of the Big Island. Our Hawaiian boy, William Wallace Blaisdell, was born on Oahu, but his home is now on the island of Molokai.

MY HOME IS ON HAWAII

by Indira Karma Hale

I SAW THE VOLCANOES ERUPT

I live on the big island of Hawaii, which is the most southerly of them all. Our home is on the Kona Coast and is not far from the volcano of Kilauea, which has been very active lately. It began to erupt in November 1959 and continued for some time afterwards. In February 1960 the lava streams reached the little village of Kapoko and burst through the earth dikes the people had put up to protect their homes. Scores of houses were burned, including the school and the courthouse.

Of course, it was a wonderful sight and all the roads were jammed with cars. The airplanes ran taxi flights over the volcano to see it.

When I was a small child I saw the lava flow from Mauna Loa during the 1950 eruption. The flow came within three hundred yards of my house, and my mother took many pictures of it. We were the first family in the vicinity to come back to live. I remember the smell of the sulphur and the sight of the glowing lava. There was another eruption on the other side of the island in 1955. My mother saw one cone of this eruption come up in the cane fields.

OUR HOUSE FACES THE SEA

We have a lovely view of the Kona Coast, which is on the southwest side of the island. On clear days we can see two other Hawaiian islands, Maui and Molokai. We have a one-story ranch-type home. The house is half cement and half logs of ohia wood. This is a native wood that is light brown in color. It is very acid and the termites won't touch it. It isn't used very much for building purposes, however, because it has to be cut and worked while it is green. Afterwards it gets far too hard.

Our house has about six rooms and a *lanai*, which is the Hawaiian word for "porch" or "patio." We have no water system so we catch rain water from our roofs and run it into two cement tanks which we clean out every five years or so. After the lava flow of 1950 the water was very dirty. We have a fireplace in our living room and in the winter we use it a good deal, since the temperature here drops to below 50° Fahrenheit.

THE NAMES IN OUR FAMILY

My mother likes to give names to things and I have inherited that from her. We call our house *Hale Laulea.* Hale is my family name, but it is also the Hawaiian word for "house." *Laulea* means "restful." But in Hawaii we pronounce these words like *ha-lay la-oo-lay-a.*

I was named by my parents Indira Karma. My parents are great admirers of Nehru, and I was named for his daughter, Mrs. Indira Gandhi. *Karma* is a common word in Hinduism and Buddhism and means rather loosely "destiny."

I was born sixteen years ago in New York City. When I was two years old we moved to San Diego in California. We stayed there for one and a half years when we moved to the

Kona district of Hawaii. I was almost four then. At that time there were only five families living near us.

My father's name is William Jennings Hale, Jr. He was born in Nashville, Tennessee, where his father was the president of the Agricultural and Industrial Institute of Tennessee. My father taught for two or three years in the South. Then he wandered around taking many kinds of jobs in different places. Finally he landed in New York City, where I was born. In New York I contracted pneumonia, so the family moved to the warmer climate of California and lived on a farm in San Diego. But even this climate was too cold. At that time there was a poet named Don Blanding who lived in California and wrote lovely poems about the Kona Coast on the island of Hawaii. Finally the family decided to move there and they chose the Kona Coast, because they had had enough of cities and wanted to go to a warm and beautiful land. My father is now teaching in an elementary school at Honaunau, about twenty miles away from our home.

My mother's name is Helene Eleanor Hilyer. She was born in Minneapolis, Minnesota, and like my father is a teacher by profession. She taught English at San Diego State College, and when she first came to Hawaii she taught at Konawaena in our local high school.

I have one brother, William Jasper Kona Hale, III. He is only three.

THE MID-PACIFIC INSTITUTE

I went to kindergarten at Konawaena when I was four. After a year and a half there I went to a number of different schools for a number of different reasons. Finally I entered the Mid-Pacific Institute at Honolulu, which is on the island of Oahu. I have been there for three years now. This school is in the Manoa Valley about five or six miles away from Honolulu,

and has about four hundred boys and girls in it, all of them boarders.

I am studying English, Latin, American history, chemistry, algebra, and physical education. The last we have twice a week and this year I am taking tennis. But I love to swim and to play Ping-pong. Indoors I play chess. Twice a week I have to do my laundry.

MY CLUBS

There are a number of clubs at the school and I belong to three of them. I am president of the Lima Kokua Society, which in Hawaiian means the "helping hand." We hold a bazaar every year, and we sell cookies and Christmas cards and other things. With the money we earn we help to support a child in Korea through the Save the Children Federation.

I belong also to the Pacific and Asian Affairs Club, and to the Triangle Y-Teen. The former studies the problems of the Pacific area, and the latter engages in the usual Y.W.C.A. activities.

THE DAILY ROUTINE

I rise in the morning at six fifteen, and I am the bell ringer for the girls' dormitory. Most of us sleep two in a room, but a few of the seniors have single rooms. They are called senators, and are responsible for discipline. They make the rules by which we have to live. There are about 170 girls they have to look out for.

Before I have my breakfast I have to do some janitorial work, cleaning the dormitories and the immediate area. We have breakfast at seven fifteen, usually pancakes, bacon and eggs, toast, fruit juices, and fruit. I drink milk. After breakfast is over, the senators inspect our rooms.

Classes come from eight ten to twelve. Then we have lunch,

sometimes soup and stew, curries, and almost always rice. From one to two thirty we have two more classes.

I am a member of the Dining Room Council, in charge of the activities of the dining hall. Dinner usually comes at six. This is about the same as our lunch. Afterwards we study from seven thirty to nine fifteen, and about nine thirty I go to bed.

SATURDAYS AND SUNDAYS

Saturday I am allowed to go into town. I usually go in the afternoon after lunch. In Honolulu I shop, roller-skate, swim, and go to the movies. Back at school in the afternoon I study and sew. Often in the evening we have dances and class parties and plays.

On Sunday church at ten is compulsory. My school was started by the Congregationalists, but it is now undenominational. After church I am quite free again. I can go to town if I want to, but this is the time when I usually go to the beach for a swim.

EXCITING THINGS

Exciting things have happened at the school all year. I have been on the honor roll. I am also on the principal's list, which is higher still. I have been back to the mainland three times since we came out here to live.

VACATIONS AT HOME

I go home for Christmas, Easter, and the long vacations. Unfortunately when I am home my father is often very busy, while he is often free when I am back in school. I do a good deal of baby-sitting during vacation and I help on our coffee plantation. Kona is one of the four places in the United States that grow coffee commercially and about three-quarters of the people are in this work. But the industry is dying since it gets no government help. The coffee is strong and is used in mixtures. My father has ten acres of it, and I have helped with the planting, the fertilizing, and the picking. It takes three years for the trees to bear.

POLITICS

Both my father and mother are much interested in politics and are firm Democrats. My mother is now a supervisor in the County of Hawaii, the first woman to hold that position. Every other week she drives over to Hilo for an official meeting. She does a lot of speaking, and when she is campaigning I help her on the social side by providing some of the entertainment.

I speak "pigeon" besides my English. "Pigeon" is the lingo of the islands. It is mostly English, but it includes also some Japanese, Hawaiian, Chinese, and Filipino words. All the island children speak it. My blood is very mixed. I am partly Indian, partly French, partly Negro, and partly Scottish. That's the way it is with many of us here.

MY HOME IS ON MOLOKAI

by William Wallace Blaisdell

I was born fifteen years ago in the Queen's Hospital at Honolulu. At that time my family was living in Kapahulu, a suburb of Honolulu. My mother was a stewardess on the Hawaiian Airlines. My father was then a fire captain and had been one for almost fifteen years.

When I was a year old we moved to Kailua, which is about sixteen miles from downtown Honolulu, between Diamond Head and Koko Head.

AN EXCITING EXPERIENCE

I had a very exciting experience there when I was about four years old. My father kept a bar at that time and one night he brought home in a box $2,000 in cash, which he put next to the window in the room where my brother and I slept. Later in the evening, after we had gone to bed, my father told an older brother to get the cash box for him. When this brother came into our room he saw a hand reaching through the window where the glass had been cut out to get the box. My brother screamed, I woke up, and my father and mother came running in. When they saw what had happened my father got his .45 caliber revolver and my mother got a knife. They started to chase the thief, but they could not catch him. He got away in the dark.

I lived at Kailua until I was seven, in a single concrete house of three rooms. Most of the people in Kailua worked in Honolulu or at Pearl Harbor.

MY PARENTS

My father was Charles Timmy Blaisdell. He was Hawaiian-Caucasian. His grandfather came from the mainland. My mother's name is Leolani. Both of my parents had been married before and both had had children. My mother had a boy named Ernest, who is now going to college on the mainland. He is twenty-two. My father had two daughters, Rosella and Moyna, who are both married now. In their second marriage my parents had two more boys, my younger brother Sumner, who is now fourteen, and myself. Sumner is now in the ninth grade of my school.

I had my first airplane ride with my mother when I was six. I was afraid, and my mother had to chase me around the airport and catch me before she could get me on board. Then we flew to the island of Molokai and I stayed there for two weeks with an aunt of mine who lived there. Afterwards I took a number of plane rides with my mother, to the big island of Hawaii and the smaller islands of Kauai and Maui. As a matter of fact, I have been almost everywhere on the islands.

Later my father died and my mother gave up her work for the airlines. She became a practical nurse, and at the present moment is taking care of a cripple on Molokai. So that is my home now.

MY SCHOOL LIFE

I went to school first of all at Kailua. This was a nursery school and I was there for a year. Then I went to St. Anthony's, which was not far from the airport, for two years. Then I went to Kamehameha School, where I have been for eight years. I am now in the tenth grade.

I am studying biology, geometry, Latin, and English. These are all called "solid" subjects, and I have each of them for five periods a week. Then I have other subjects which are not "solid": military science, drill, physical education, music, and shop. In shop I study woodwork, metalwork, and agriculture.

I like best of all my geometry, and I want to go on to college. I should like to study aeronautical engineering at the Massachusetts Institute of Technology in Cambridge, Massachusetts.

There are about seventeen hundred pupils at the Kamehameha School. It really consists of three schools: a boys' school of five hundred pupils, a girls' school of five hundred pupils, and a preparatory school of about seven hundred pupils. These schools are all separated, but the boys and girls get together for proms and other social activities.

From the ninth grade to the twelfth grade the boys have R.O.T.C. training. There is nothing equivalent for the girls.

The boys have dormitories with about thirty rooms in each. Every boy has his own room. When the bugle sounds at six, we all get up. By six twenty we must be dressed and in our ranks for the salute to the colors. Breakfast is at six thirty, and we eat cereal, bacon and eggs or sausage, doughnuts or rolls, fruit, and cocoa. At six fifty we break up into work squads and work until seven fifteen cleaning the dormitories, the gym, the classrooms, and the grounds, and washing the dishes. Then we take off our fatigues and get into our khaki uniforms.

Classes begin at seven forty-five and last until eleven. At eleven ten we have lunch: meat loaf, salad, vegetables, and dessert. We have milk to drink. From eleven thirty till twelve five we rest or do whatever we please. Then there are classes again from twelve five to three twenty, when school is over. The day students then go home, and the rest of us are free. Sometimes we iron our clothes, sometimes we play baseball or football. At five forty we must be in uniform again for inspection and the salute to the flag. Then we have dinner.

For dinner we have lamb or some other meat or fish, vegetables, salad, and for dessert, pie or pudding or ice cream. We drink milk. My favorite dish is *teriyaki* steak, which is "steak flavored with onions and ginger." I like lamb also.

Six thirty to seven is a free period when we just fool around. From seven to eight forty-five we study in the study hall, and taps sound at nine. From nine to ten we may study if we want to, but we don't have to. At ten we go to bed.

WEEKENDS AND VACATIONS

On Saturday we boarders have inspection at eight ten and then we are free to go into the city if we want to. We can go to the movies or the beaches or watch a football game. We often have lunch in town, but we must be back at five thirty. Dinner comes at six, and sometimes we have football games at the school in the evening; sometimes, entertainment, dances, and proms. The seniors can bring dates from the town, but the rest of us have to take the girls from the school.

On Sundays we are free from seven thirty to nine. From nine thirty to ten thirty the ninth-graders must go to Sunday School, but the rest of the school stay in the rooms until ten thirty, when we all go to chapel, boys and girls together. There are many different kinds of religion at the school, and we have two chaplains.

Dinner comes at twelve thirty, and from one to five thirty we are completely free. We can take the swimming bus to the beaches, or we can call at the girls' school. Then from seven to eight in the evening we study, from eight to eight fifteen we get ready for bed, from eight fifteen to nine we are free in our rooms, and at nine we are in bed.

We have five days' vacation at Thanksgiving, two weeks at Christmas, a long four-day weekend in February, a week at Easter, and a long vacation in the summer from the end of May until early in September.

LIFE ON MOLOKAI

My mother is taking care of a cripple on Molokai, and that is what I call my home. Of course, I spend all my vacations there. The capital of Molokai is Kaunakakai on the southern shore. It is the biggest town and has about fifteen hundred people in it. The island is a great place for pineapples. The pineapples are shipped to Honolulu to be canned.

There isn't much to do on Molokai for a boy. But I swim and fish and play football and basketball. There is good camping in the mountains, and I go there for a few days at a time. The deer hunting is very good also.

On the north shore of the island is the famous colony of lepers, where the Belgian priest Father Damien worked and died, but we have to get special permission to visit it.

I AM PRESIDENT OF MY CLASS

At school only the seniors can be officers of the R.O.T.C., but I am the president of my tenth-grade class, which is the sophomore class. I am also in the top ten of my class. I wear a blue braid over my left shoulder on my uniform to show that I belong to the best company among the school cadets, and on the shoulder strap I wear the school insignia, which is blue and white, with the word *kamoi*, which means "king," on it.

GOOD TIMES AT SCHOOL

We have lots of good times at our school. For instance, we have a *hoolaulea*, which means an "open house." Then all the three schools are open. The drill team performs; we have an athletic exhibition, a baseball game, and a big *luau*, or Hawaiian feast, on the grounds. The people buy tickets.

Founders Day is on December 19. This day is in honor of the two people who founded our school. King Kamehameha began to rule in the middle of the eighteenth century, and the last of that line of native princesses was Bernice Pauahi, who married an American named Bishop. These two people founded the school. When we first enter the school we all pledge to honor the memory of our benefactress, Bernice Pauahi Bishop, and to uphold her ideals. Boys and girls of Hawaiian descent have preference when they apply for admission. Boarders have to pay $130.00 a year. Day students pay $60.00.

Once a year the public is invited to a song contest among the classes. The seniors usually win.

We have a public parade about once a month.

HAWAIIAN

At school everyone calls me Willie. I speak English, of course, and Hawaiian also. Most everyone, except the *haole*, who is the "newcomer" on the island, speaks Hawaiian. Some people learn it more easily than others. They are *akamai*, or "smart," as we say. The others, we say, are *lolo*, or "dumb." *Aloha* is the word we use for both greetings and farewells. *Pau* means "finish," and this is *pau* for my story.

3. THE SOCIETY ISLANDS

AN ENCHANTED WORLD

A NEVER-NEVER LAND

For painters and poets, for adventurers and vagabonds, for writers and explorers, for traders and tourists, the Society Islands have always been a kind of never-never land, the place of sunshine and balmy air, the home of eternal spring, where lovely maidens with crowns of flowers in their hair danced on coral strands under palm trees laden with milky fruit.

AN UPSIDE-DOWN COUNTRY

We are now in the Southern Hemisphere. You may forget sometimes that if you are to look in the direction of these islands you mustn't look to the west or the southwest but down through the earth under your feet. Most of the countries we are to visit are "down under," which is the way the people of Australia and New Zealand locate their homes. If you were to draw a big circle on a paper to represent the earth the islands we are talking about would have to be shown lying upside down with their coconut trees waving their fronds downward, and the people walking with their feet above their heads like flies on a ceiling.

THE PLANET VENUS

In the early summer of 1769 the planet Venus was to pass over the face of the sun. The astronomers in England knew about this, but they could not see it happen in England itself. A certain Captain Samuel Wallis, whom King George III had sent to the South Seas, had just returned to England. He reported that the best place to see the transit of Venus across the disk of the sun was an island which he had named King George III, but which the natives called Otaheite. The Royal Society for Improving Natural Knowledge had been founded in London a hundred years before. This society wanted very much to have scientific observations of this important celestial event. So they asked the James Cook who was killed later in Hawaii to take a group of scientists to this island to watch the crossing of Venus there. The ship Cook commanded was called the *Endeavour*, and it took him eight months of sailing to reach Otaheite. Then he spent three very happy months on the island among the natives and explored other islands in the vicinity. The natives became very fond of him. One of their chiefs changed his name from Oree to Cookee in his honor.

Meanwhile the scientists observed the transit of Venus and Cook renamed the islands in honor of the Royal Society. Ever since we have called them the Society Islands.

But the island of Otaheite, which we now call Tahiti, he called the Beloved Island. Altogether Cook visited these islands three times. On his last visit he rode on horseback. This astounded the natives, who had never seen a horse before. Was this creature one animal or two? they wondered.

There is a beacon on Venus Point in Tahiti now in memory of Captain Cook.

THE MUTINY ON THE BOUNTY

One of the most famous incidents in the history of the Society Islands was the mutiny on *His Majesty's Ship Bounty*, commanded by Captain William Bligh. It was in 1789. The *Bounty* had gone to Tahiti to get a cargo of breadfruit trees that were to be carried to the West Indies. Shortly after the *Bounty* left the island the majority of the crew mutinied. They set Captain Bligh with eighteen of his faithful followers adrift in a small boat. This boat sailed four thousand miles and reached the East Indies safely. It was an amazing feat of navigation and endurance.

Meanwhile the mutineers returned to Tahiti. Later some of them sailed away to little rocky Pitcairn Island. You can still find descendants of the mutineers there today.

FRENCH POLYNESIA

French Polynesia is an overseas territory of the French Republic. The Society Islands are just one group in Eastern French Polynesia, which numbers at least 130 islands scattered over a million square miles of the Pacific. This is about the area of the whole of Western Europe. There are a number of separate archipelagoes. The Society Islands themselves consist of two groups. Tahiti belongs to the Windward Islands, which lie in the direction of the southeast trade winds. The other group is the Leeward Islands, of which Borabora is perhaps the best known. They lie away from the direction of the trades.

About eight hundred miles to the northeast are the ten high islands of the Marquesas Archipelago. To the south are the five high Austral Islands from three hundred to seven hundred miles away. To the east and southeast is the Tuamotu

Archipelago with eighty-two coral islands, and the ten small islands of the Gambiers.

THE LOW ISLANDS

The high islands are volcanic in origin, like the Hawaiian Islands. Here in French Polynesia there are many high islands, but there are low ones too. Most of the Tuamotus are low islands. These islands are built by tiny invertebrates, or animals that have no spinal columns, called polyps. The polyps take lime from the sea water and fashion houses for themselves out of it. Then they attach themselves to other polyps in the masses we call coral. When the polyps die the shells they have built for themselves remain, and new generations of living polyps attach themselves to these tiny abandoned houses.

Polyps can live only in salt water, so the coral islands never rise much above sea level. They like fairly warm water too, so that they seldom live more than 130 feet below the surface. On the island of Bikini much farther north in Micronesia, however, men have drilled down for 2,500 feet and have found coral all the way. But all the coral was dead at this depth, and probably had sunk in some past earthquake.

Coral has a great variety of forms and many beautiful colors: red, pink, green, yellow, blue, and cream. The dead coral we usually see is white, but live coral is never white.

Just off the northeastern coast of Australia is the Great Barrier Reef. It's 1,260 miles long and it's all coral. There are many smaller reefs of coral in other parts of the Pacific. The polyps are the world's greatest builders.

Often the coral island is formed like a ring around a quiet central lagoon. Then it's called an atoll. It's possible that the reef was once attached to a high island, which afterwards sank into the sea, leaving the atoll behind. Sometimes the atolls, however, are very irregular, not in the form of a circle at all. There are usually openings in the reefs that allow ships to enter into the quiet lagoon. These lagoons are sometimes very large. Eniwetok, north in the Micronesian Islands, has a lagoon that is twenty miles in diameter.

The beaches of these islands in the South Pacific are composed of crushed coral. Not much can grow in this kind of soil, but the coconut thrives there. It sends its roots deep down and finds in brackish water all the nourishment it needs.

LIFE IS PLEASANT ON THE ISLANDS

Life on these islands of French Polynesia is very easy. The people fish, dive for pearl oysters, and gather *bêches-de-mer*, or "sea slugs." The last are considered delicacies by the Oriental peoples. The natives gather coconuts also and dry the meat to get copra, which is used for making soap and other things. Phosphates are found on one island, coffee is grown on Tahiti, and vanilla on Mooréa. Tourism is, of course, an important business.

The natives have a "festive Polynesian meal" they call a *tamaaraa*. An "underground oven" called a *himaa* is filled with stones which are heated by building a fire over them. Then the food is put on to cook: always a suckling pig, but also fish, vegetables, sweet potatoes, and breadfruit. The food is covered with leaves and sacking, and it takes about two hours to cook.

Whenever there is *tamaaraa* there is almost always dancing. The men and women wear garlands of flowers, and the dancing is very beautiful. Often the dancers portray incidents in the history of the islands, like the long voyages on the open sea that brought them to their present homes.

Both of our young people live on Tahiti in the Society Islands. Jacques Mariterage lives just outside of Papeete, the capital. His father is a sailor for the Mormons, a religious sect which is strong in these parts, and Jacques has visited with him many of the Polynesian islands we have mentioned. Michelle Tavaite Bordes lives in Taravao, a village which is about thirty-five miles south of Papeete. Her father grows coffee and keeps cattle and goats for their milk and meat.

I LIVE ON BIG TAHITI

by Jacques Mariterage

BIG AND LITTLE TAHITI

Tahiti looks on the map a little like a dumbbell. The biggest part is called *Tahiti-Nui,* which means "Big Tahiti." The small part is called *Tahiti-Iti,* which means "Little Tahiti." The two parts are connected by a narrow neck of land. I was born at Tabuai, which is south of Papeete, the capital, and in the center of the island. At that time my father was a farmer there. He had a coffee plantation and sold the coffee beans.

BRITTLE MOUNTAINS

The interior of my island is very mountainous. One of the mountains is Arohena, and it is 7,000 feet high. Aorai is not quite so high, but there is a road that goes almost up to the top. People go up to see the view over my island of Tahiti and the nearby island of Mooréa. Another mountain is called Diadem, because the top of it looks like a crown. Some of these mountains have never been climbed, not because they are so high, but because the rock is very brittle. That makes climbing dangerous.

MY HOUSE AT FAUTAUA

I stayed with my family on the farm until I was six years old. Then we moved to a place called Fautaua, which is a town near Papeete. That's where I've lived ever since.

My house is one big room, with walls of wood panels and a corrugated iron roof. There is a space under the eaves for ventilation and there are windows on all four sides. The room is about thirty by thirty feet and there are beds in all the corners of it. We cook in the open outside the house.

All around the house is a grove of bananas and coconuts. We have pineapples too. There are many other houses like this around ours, but we can see very few of them because the bananas are growing so thickly there.

MY FATHER IS A SAILOR FOR THE MORMONS

My father's name is Robert, and he was born on one of the Tuamotu Islands. There are about eighty of them and they cover many square miles of ocean. Most of them are just low reefs. They get lots of phosphates from these islands.

My father does not farm now except to take care of the fruit trees around our house. He is now the first mate of a boat that belongs to the Church of the Latter-day Saints. The boat is called the *Paraita*, and is named for the first Mormon missionary who came to these islands more than one hundred years ago. The boat is a big sail boat, and the church uses it to visit the other islands where there are missions, to take them supplies, and to carry people to conferences. I have often been on the boat with my father, so I have visited a good many of the Polynesian Islands to which the Society Islands belong.

My mother is Tehinatearo and she was born at Tubuai. I have two sisters and two brothers. The oldest is my sister Noeline. She is fourteen and goes to the same school I go to. I am thirteen. Alfred is nine and is in the fourth class. My sister Monique is six, and the youngest, Jean, is three.

SCHOOL DAYS

I first went to school when I was five, and I am now in the second class of the secondary school. The school is called the Mamao School. It is a fine modern building in that part of Papeete called Mamao.

I have French, arithmetic, natural science, history, and geography. We don't have a gym at the school, and there are no organized sports there. I like my science best, and I want to be a mechanic.

I get up at five and have bread and tea for breakfast. Before I go to school I play outside for a little while. School is some distance away from the house and I go there on foot. There are both morning and afternoon sessions. Classes in the morning are from seven thirty to eleven. Then I walk home for lunch. Sometimes we have fish, salad, and fruit, with lemonade to drink. Sometimes we have meat. I go back to school in the afternoon from one to four. Then I go home again, take a bath, and help my mother get supper. This comes at six and is about the same as our lunch, though we sometimes have soup. After supper I do my homework for half an hour and listen to the radio. I often go out to play football too, but I never play any indoor games.

On Saturday we have school all day, so it's about the same as any other day in the week.

I AM A DEACON IN MY CHURCH

On Sunday I go to the Sunday School at nine o'clock. This is at the Church of the Latter Day Saints. I am a deacon at the church, so at ten thirty I go to the priesthood meeting. There I learn how to pass the sacraments and I study the gospels. We have older leaders for this meeting. In the afternoon I play football and tennis. Sometimes, too, I go on picnics with my family to the shore. I fish often from a boat there.

Our long vacation comes from July 10 to October 1. During these weeks I work among our fruit trees and I read a great deal. I can borrow books from my school for vacation reading.

Our big holiday here is the fourteenth of July. As a matter of fact, the holiday often lasts for a week or two. We have parades and boat races and many dances, both day and night. The other islands send dance groups and we have a dancing contest to see which is the best. Everyone who can go to Papeete then goes. Almost no business is done, and the whole island is a kind of big playground.

I COME FROM LITTLE TAHITI

by Michelle Tavaite Bordes

MY FATHER IS A COFFEE GROWER

I was born fourteen years ago at Taravao, on Tahiti-Iti, which is Little Tahiti. Of course, the whole island of Tahiti is small, and my home is only about thirty-five miles from Papeete. We live near the little neck of land between the two parts of the island. Taravao is rather an important village, mostly agricultural, but we don't live in the center of it. We live on the top of a plateau above the village, where we can see almost the whole of the two parts of the island. My father has a big coffee plantation there, and every year he exports from twelve to fourteen tons of coffee by the steamers of the Messageries Maritimes.

My house there is of wood with an iron roof. It has four rooms, all on one floor, with a kitchen in a small separate building. We use gasoline lamps in our house and we get our water from a river that comes down from the mountains and runs by the house.

There is another building also for the three men my father hires all the year round. When the coffee-harvesting time comes, however, we have to have about fifty workers, many of them women. For these workers who stay on the plantation for two months my father has to have still another big house. The men and women bring their food from home and prepare it themselves, but they sleep on the plantation.

We have about twenty cows and we sell both the milk and the meat. Then we have a herd of one hundred goats. We buy the goats on another island called Mehetia, which is a day's boat journey away. From time to time I go there to bring back goats for my father. This boat belongs to my uncle and is called the *Eameo*.

My father's name is François Teharee. He was born in Taravao, but not in the house where we now live. He has always tended the same coffee grove, and his father did before him.

MY MOTHER WAS BORN ON MOORÉA

My mother was born on Mooréa, the nearest island to Tahiti. Some people say that this is the most beautiful island in the world. It is really very lovely with tall, jagged mountain peaks, two lovely bays, one of them named for the old explorer Captain James Cook, and many coconut groves. My mother was born in the fishing village of Afareaitu on the eastern coast. The people on Mooréa grow the vanilla vine and prepare the pods to sell. They also make copra from the coconut.

I have two sisters. One is called Heipua, which means a wreath or a crown made of the flower called *pua*. She is eleven and goes to the school I attend. The other sister is Vaihere. Her name means "much loved water." She lives with my mother's sister in Papeete.

HORSEBACK AT FOUR

When I was small there were no children at all around my house to play with, so I had to amuse myself. I used to climb trees. My father had one horse and I used to ride horseback when I was four. I gathered oranges also. We had a banana grove too, but it takes two men to cut down the big bunches of bananas. Then when I got older and was at home I used to milk the cows and take care of the goats.

SCHOOL AT PAPEETE

When I was four years old my father sent me to Papeete to begin my schooling. I first went to the infants' class at the Collège Anne-Marie Javouhey. I lived with my aunt who is a teacher. After the infant class I went to primary school and I am now in the fourth class of the Collège.

My school is named for one of the greatest missionaries of the Catholic Church, who founded the Congregation of St. Joseph of Cluny. Anne-Marie Javouhey was a peasant girl, born on a French farm. She gave her life for the dark-skinned people of the world. There are now four thousand nuns of every race working in many parts of the world. And there are scores of houses of this order in French Oceania.

At this school I am now studying French, English, Spanish, history, geography, mathematics, physics, chemistry, and religion. We do not have physical education of any kind.

I think I like mathematics best and I want to be a teacher.

THE DAY BEGINS

My day begins at five thirty. I sometimes go to Mass and sing in the choir, and sometimes I study before breakfast. For breakfast I have bread and butter and *café au lait*. Then I have twenty minutes to help clean the dormitories and the classrooms. Lessons are from seven thirty to eleven thirty and then I have lunch, when we have meat and vegetables and fruit. After lunch every day I study the piano. We have more classes from one thirty to four. Then after I eat a little snack, I go outdoors to play a while. The girls here all like to juggle four lemons and I do that too. I jump and run. Then

I study for two hours before I have my dinner, which is the same as my lunch except that I have soup. I go out to play for a while in the evening too, and indoors I embroider. We have two dormitories, each of them for forty-five girls.

On Sunday I go to Mass in the cathedral at eight, where I sing in the choir. Then I read a good deal. We have radios in our classrooms but not in our dormitories. Sometimes we go to the movies, but we also have movies occasionally in our classes.

HOME AT TARAVAO

The long vacation is from July 10 to October 1, and then, of course, I go home to Taravao. There I help my mother and work on the farm. But I have lots of fun too, and now there are other girls to play with. I play badminton and croquet with them, I swim in the sea, and I paddle an outrigger canoe. My father has a jeep and we often go on nice picnics. Sometimes we drive to that part of Little Tahiti called the Tautira. There is no road around the southeastern side of the island, but in a canoe we can visit the Pari and see the many waterfalls tumbling down the steep ravines into the sea. There are really hundreds of them.

At Papeete on Bastille Day and the days that follow there are all kinds of games and fun for the young people, mostly in the square in front of the post office.

I speak Tahitian and French and I am learning Spanish and English.

4. THE COOK ISLANDS

THE FORMER SAVAGE ISLANDS

THE SAVAGE ISLANDS

After the Polynesians had lived for some time on Otaheite, but long before James Cook had visited them and rechristened them the Society Islands, some of the big canoes sailed westward to find still another home in the vast Pacific. They landed on a group of islands almost 700 miles away, which we know now as the Cook Islands. Almost 800 miles still farther west was Western Samoa, 1,200 miles away was Fiji, and 1,500 miles away was New Zealand. There were fifteen islands in their new home, covering about 84 square miles, but scattered over an ocean area of 800,000 square miles. Today there are about 12,500 people on them.

Europeans knew nothing about these islands at that time. Some of them were discovered by James Cook in 1773. When he approached the shore he was greeted with a shower of stones and spears. So he called them the Savage Islands. Farther west he visited the Tonga Islands. There the people were so hospitable that he called them, on the contrary, the Friendly Islands.

CAPTAIN BLIGH OF THE BOUNTY

In 1789 Captain William Bligh left Otaheite, where his men had been very happy with the dusky maidens, and set sail to the west with his cargo of breadfruit. He was not expecting to find any islands in this part of the ocean, and so he was much surprised when on April 11 he sighted an uncharted island which he wrote "was of moderate height with a round conical hill toward the northern extreme of it." This was certainly the island we now know as Aitutaki. He also wrote, "A number of small keys were seen from the masthead lying to the southeast, and at noon we could count nine of them. They were all covered with trees and the large island had the most fruitful appearance. The shore was bordered by flat land with innumerable coconuts and other trees and the high grounds were beautiful interspersed with lawns. I could not near the shore on account of the wind, nevertheless there appeared broken water between all the keys, and I am inclined to think they are all joined by a reef. I saw no smoke or any sign of inhabitants, it is scarcely to be imagined, however, that so charming a little spot is without them."

Probably these keys were around the lagoon where Aitutaki is situated.

It was two weeks later that Captain Bligh was set adrift by his mutinous sailors.

The islands are no longer called the Savage Islands. We know them today as the Cook Islands.

TWO MAJOR ISLAND GROUPS

There are two main groups, one in the north and one in the south. The northern group consists of seven islands: Penrhyn, Manihiki, Rakahanga, Pukapuka, Suwarrow, Nassau, and Palmerston. These are all low islands like those in the Tuamotu Archipelago in French Polynesia. They are coral atolls and depend on copra and pearl shells for their support.

MISTER MARSTERS

One of these atolls, Palmerston, has had a very interesting history. It's a lovely island, one of the most beautiful in the world. Many people have dreamed of retiring to this island and living out their days in peace there. In an irregular circle are six islands strung on the necklace of a coral reef. The sheltered lagoon inside is exquisite with its palette of rainbow colors.

This lonely atoll is remote from the others. It was discovered by Cook on June 16, 1774. He named it for Lord Palmerston, one of the Lords of the Admiralty at that time. On his third voyage Cook called once again to get water and fish and coconuts. His men found no life on the atoll, just the remains of a battered canoe.

Then in 1862 a new and strange chapter in the history of the island began. A William Marsters from Gloucestershire, England, came to manage the island for a trader. He seemed to have had three wives and by each of them he raised a large family. The trader disappeared. In 1892 the British Crown gave Marsters a lease of the island. By that time the population numbered one hundred. Marsters insisted on everyone speaking English, which seemed strange to visitors who thought they were in Polynesia. He died in 1899.

Then came his eldest son, William Marsters the Second, who died in 1946. Another head of the family succeeded him. The Marsters men sometimes went to Aitutaki and other islands to find wives.

Life has not always been idyllic in this lovely place. In 1883 all the coconut palms were destroyed by a big storm. Again in 1914, 1923, 1926, 1931, and 1935 other hurricanes came, blowing away most of the homes and laying all the crops low. Some of the people then moved away, but others still cling to their little island world.

About once a year a ship arrives from New Zealand with supplies.

RAROTONGA

The southern group of islands are Rarotonga, Aitutaki, Atiu, Mitiaro, Mauke, and Manuae. These islands are volcanic, but there have been no eruptions within the memory of the people living on them.

The most important of them is Rarotonga, which is the administrative center for the whole group. It's the largest island and the highest. From the midst of low hills, which are only a few hundred feet high, rises a three-thousand-foot mountain.

The people depend on fish and fruit and vegetables for their living. Copra, oranges, and tomatoes are exported.

THE GOVERNMENT

In 1888 the British government made the Cook Islands a protectorate, and annexed them in 1900. The following year they were placed under the government of New Zealand. Finally in 1907 they became with New Zealand a part of the great British Commonwealth.

Our two youthful Cook Islanders live on Aitutaki, the most northerly of the southern group. You will be interested to hear about Teretai Ioane Peneka and his "feeding father," who is a fisherman and a farmer. You will also like to know Repeta Kaitao, whose father is one of the eight policemen on the island. She wants to be a teacher and will certainly go to Rarotonga to study.

I HAVE A FEEDING FATHER

by Teretai Ioane Peneka

MY FEEDING FATHER

I was born in Rarotonga, which is the capital of the Cook Islands, twelve years ago, but I lived there for only seven or eight months before my family moved to Aitutaki, the most northerly of the Cook Islands. We all came in a boat, which is the only way one can come. When I was seven or eight years old my father, whose name was Ioane Peneka, died. He was a fisherman and a farmer.

Now I have a feeding father, whose name is Ngere Maea. He is my grandmother's second husband, but he is also my feeding father. It is the custom here to give the first-born boy to the grandfather. Often the boy will take his feeding father's name, but I didn't do that. The other children in a family may also have feeding fathers who become responsible for them. In fact a child can change its feeding father three or four times, and each time take a new name. So the village records are often very mixed up. A child's own father always has the right to take the child back again.

My feeding father is a fisherman and a farmer.

I LIVE ON AITUTAKI

I live in the little village of Tautu which is about one and a half miles from the administrative center of Aitutaki. There are about 150 people that live there, and the place is right on the shore. Most of the people are fishermen or farmers, but there are some men who have jobs at the airport. When the Americans were here on the island during the war they built an airport but it is only used by government planes. We have no hotels here, and tourists never come, unless by accident when the planes break down. The Tasman Empire Airlines used to land here on the way to Tahiti in a flying boat, which came down on the water of our big lagoon and refueled at another of the islands around the lagoon, called Akaiami. Only one man, the caretaker, lived on Akaiami. The plane only stayed for an hour or so and then flew on. My island is some distance away from Akaiami.

On my island there are about 2,500 people, but only about a dozen Europeans. My ancestors probably came from Tahiti, and some of them moved on to New Zealand.

FISHING AND FARMING

There is very good fishing all around the island. We catch *taraoa*, *tangua*, *paoa*, and parrot fish. I like the *tangau* best. We catch these fish inside the reef. There are tuna fish outside the reef also, but my father never goes fishing for them. He only goes fishing to get fish for the family and there is always plenty of fish inside the lagoon. I often go fishing with my father, particularly on Saturday, so we can have fish for Sunday. But we do not go fishing every day.

The land is very fertile on Aitutaki and my father grows bananas, pineapples, sweet potatoes, arrowroot, which is [illegible]lled *pia* here, and coconuts. He dries the meat of the coco-[illegible] make copra, which he sells to the copra cooperatives. [illegible]oot of the *pia* is peeled, grated, soaked in water overnight, squeezed, dried, and cooked. It is then like a pudding and is eaten with a spoon.

OUR HOUSE HAS ONE ROOM

My house is a European house of one story. The walls are of wood and the roof of corrugated iron. There is just one big room inside and we sleep in beds. We have a separate cookhouse, where we have a Maori oven. There is a pit in the ground full of stones. We keep a fire burning on the stones until they are very hot and then we cook our food on the stones. Sometimes we spread mats over the food when we want to steam it or bake it. We eat our meals at a table, seated on benches.

We have benzine lamps and we get our water from a well. We have a horse which we use for transporting things.

THE FAMILY

My mother's name is Katai William. William is her father's name. She has married again and lives in the same village. My own father had eight children, but two of them died. My feeding father has no children.

The first in the family is Takina who is twenty. She lives with me and helps with the housework. She has a twin sister who lives with my mother in the same village. My brother William comes next. He is seventeen and is a fisherman. He lives with my mother also. Rakake, my fifteen-year-old sister, lives with me. She is sick and does not go to school. Then came the two boys who died. Then I come, and after me is Williamtou, who is ten and in the sixth grade in my school. He lives with me too.

CHILDHOOD GAMES

Before I went to school I used to play football and sail boats with the other boys. We played *pua* also. This is played with a big round wooden disk. We wind a string around the disk and send it spinning along the road. I played jackstones, and I think it was the American soldiers who first taught us to play this game.

THE ARAURA SCHOOL

When I was six I started my schooling at the Araura School. A very long time ago Aitutaki used to be called Araura.

My school is at Arutunga, the administrative center, and is the largest school on the island. It has 650 boys and girls. We all wear uniforms at school. The girls wear khaki skirts and white blouses. The boys wear khaki shorts and no tops. Neither the boys nor the girls usually wear shoes.

In the first two grades in my school all the teaching is in Maori. In the later grades almost all the teaching is in English.

I have social studies (civics, history, and geography), arithmetic, English, physical education, singing, art, woodwork, and health. We have a school farm, and the government has planted peanuts on it, which is a new crop for our island. The boys play Rugby, and both boys and girls play basketball and softball.

Of all my studies I like art best, but later I should like to work for the government in public health.

I'M UP WITH THE SUN

I get up as soon as the sun does. This may be at five or six. My breakfast consists of vegetables, bread, and tea. After that I feed the pigs and chickens and go to school on foot. It takes me about thirty minutes to get there. School lasts from seven fifty to one. At ten we have a fifteen-minute break and another break from eleven fifty to twelve. I bring some mangoes to school with me for a snack and the school provides milk. At one ten we have a ten-minute assembly. Then I walk home.

For lunch I have fish, vegetables, pineapples, or papaws.

I drink coconut milk or tea. Sometimes we have meat. In the afternoon I work on the farm until five when I have a swim. My dinner is the same as my lunch. Then I do homework for a half-hour and go to bed about seven.

We have no school on Saturday. Usually twice that day I go fishing with my father. We have an outrigger canoe with a sail, and we cast or troll for our fish. We do not sell any that we catch. We eat them all. On Saturdays I read a good deal, too, books I bring home from school.

THE LONDON MISSIONARY SOCIETY

I go to the London Missionary Society church and on Sundays I attend Sunday School at eight thirty in the morning. Then I go to the preaching service. There is another service at three thirty in the afternoon. One of the deacons takes the service in the morning and the pastor takes it in the afternoon. Both of them are Cook Islanders. On Wednesday and Friday there is also a service in the church at six o'clock in the morning.

I belong to the Boys Brigade, which meets at four forty-five on Thursday. We spend a good deal of time drilling, but this is not just marching. We have physical exercises also, tumbling, pyramids, horses, and things like that. About once a month all the boys come to the London Missionary Society church for a special meeting. And on Sundays the Boys Brigade makes up a large part of the Sunday School.

HOLIDAYS

On April 25 we celebrate ANZAC Day with church services for the soldiers of both wars. ANZAC stands for Australian and New Zealand Army Corps.

We have Proclamation Day in October. This is the anniversary of the time when the island chiefs ceded the islands to New Zealand.

On Christmas Day the people from one of the villages come around the island dancing and singing and collecting money for the meetinghouse or for something like that. Every year a different village does it. We always have pork and cakes then. Friends often give presents to one another like soap, combs, and hair oil. Some families have presents for the very little ones, but we don't do that in our house.

On New Year's Day one of the villages provides dancing and singing for the others, just as on Christmas Day.

I play the drums at the school assembly, and I can play the ukulele also. I speak Maori and English.

I AM AN AITUTAKI GIRL

by Repeta Kaitao

A NATIVE-STYLE HOUSE

I was born fifteen years ago on the island of Aitutaki. This town is very near the administrative center. There are about seven villages on the island, and my village has about fifty houses in it. The people are mostly fishermen and farmers, though there are some who work in shops and some who work for the administration.

The house I live in is a native-style house with wooden walls and a thatched roof. The thatch comes from the coconut palms and every three years we have to replace it with a new roof. Our house is near the shore but the road runs between us and the beach. We have one big room in the house and we have beds to sleep on. The cookhouse is behind the main house, and we eat there. I was not born in this house, but in another house like it in the same village.

MY FATHER IS A POLICEMAN

My father's name is Kaitao Rota. He was born in the same village and he has been a policeman for nine years. There are eight policemen on the island and there is a sergeant in charge of them. When my father has time he goes fishing, but he has no farm.

My mother's name is Tungane Mokotupu. Mokotupu is her father's name. She was born on Aitutaki but in another village.

The oldest child in the family is Amiria Kaitao, who is seventeen. She is studying now in the training college at Rarotonga, which is the capital of the Cook Islands. She wants to be a teacher. After her I come and then comes Katai, a girl of thirteen, who is studying at Tereora College in Rarotonga. This is the only secondary school in the Cook Islands.

Tuskau is a boy of twelve, and he is at Amuri School on Aitutaki. Gardner, ten years old, and Kii, seven years old, are in my school, Araura. Mooroa is a boy of six. He has gone to school at Rarotonga. He and Amiria live with an aunt there. Tuaine is a boy of four. He is now living in Auckland, New Zealand, with an uncle. He has to have some special eye treatment there. Last comes Tapairu, a girl of two, who is at home.

GAMES AND STUDIES

When I was a small girl I used to swim and play marbles and jackstones. I started going to Araura School when I was five and I am still there, in the ninth grade now. I have the same subjects as Teretai, except that I have sewing instead of woodworking. I like arithmetic best and I'd like to be a teacher.

I get up at six and usually have bread and butter and tea for breakfast. Sometimes I have taro too. I help my mother wash the dishes and then I go to school, where my program is the same as Teretai's. When I have time at home I make big mats for the family from the long leaves of the pandanus tree. I collect kapok also and make mattresses and pillows from it. At night I go to bed about eight.

SATURDAYS AND SUNDAYS

On Saturdays I wash my clothes at the well and help to clean house. Saturday is cooking day also, when we prepare the food for Sunday. In the afternoon I swim and walk and play tennis. At school I play basketball and softball. Sometimes I go to the movies every week. It depends upon the program. The ships come very seldom to our island and the same film is often shown for months before it is changed. However, I sometimes go to see the same film three or four times.

On Sundays I go to the London Missionary Society Church and help my mother. At twelve there is a Sunday School for the older girls, and at three thirty I go to the second service. The rest of the day I am usually in the house.

THE GIRL GUIDES

I belong to the Girl Guides, which meet at four o'clock on Thursday and Saturday afternoons. During the long vacation which comes from the middle of December to the first of February the Girl Guides have a week's camp at the school. During this week we live at the school. I have passed knots, cooking, highway code, tracking, and a number of other things.

I sing and dance and play the ukulele. I speak Maori and English.

5. SAMOA

THE NAVIGATORS' ISLANDS

IN THE BEGINNING

An old Samoan legend tells of the time when only the sky was peopled and all below was sea. One of the heavenly gods changed his daughter into a bird and sent her down to drop a stone into the water. Where she dropped it a mountain grew. She returned to heaven and once more her father sent her back with a basket of soil and a yam plant. On her third visit she was told to pluck out some feathers and leave them. This time, when she flew back to earth she found three large islands covered with vines. The feathers she dropped became birds, and some broken sticks from the yam vines became men and women.

So Samoa was born.

THE NAVIGATORS' ISLANDS

When the first of the daring Polynesian natives arrived after what must have been many years of hard living on the little scattered atolls of the sea, they immediately fell in love with Samoa. They thought it must be the most beautiful place in the whole world. And when the early explorers arrived they shared the enthusiasm of the natives. It was an Eldorado for them. "On these islands," they thought, "are undoubtedly the happiest people of the earth!" They found the people so much at home in their outrigger canoes that the explorers began to call the islands the Navigators' Islands.

THE HEART OF THE SOUTH PACIFIC

Samoa is the most central of the South Sea island groups. It's over 4,000 miles from the United States, more than 2,000 from Hawaii, more than 1,500 from New Zealand. It's about 900 miles west of Aitutaki in the Cook Islands and 200 miles from Fiji, the next important group to the west.

The group is divided into two parts. Eastern Samoa belongs to the United States. Western Samoa, recently a trust territory administered for the United Nations by New Zealand, is now independent.

The largest island is rugged Savaii with seven hundred square miles in it. Like all the other islands it is of volcanic origin. It has few and poor anchorages for ships. Upolu is the second largest with four hundred square miles. Its gentle, wooded slopes provide good locations for homes, particularly on the northern shore, where Apia, the capital and largest city, is located. These two islands are in Western Samoa.

In Eastern Samoa the most important island is Tutuila, another rugged place, where the American port of Pago Pago (pronounced *Pahng-o Pahng-o*) is situated. The harbor there is a mile and a half long and three-quarters of a mile wide. It's really the submerged crater of a volcano, and it contains what is often called the finest port in the South Pacific. But Tutuila itself has only about seventy-five square miles, and very little land suitable for farming.

There are a number of other small islands, and most of the islands, big and little, are surrounded by coral reefs.

THE WHITES ARRIVE

The Dutch were the first of the Europeans to discover the islands. They came soon after 1700. Later Louis Antoine de Bougainville, the French explorer, visited them. Later still the Germans came and soon they had gained control of Savaii and Upolu. At first the whites were regarded as gods by the natives. They had sails on tall masts. They guided their ships with compasses, when the natives used the stars, the winds, the clouds, the currents, the fish, and the birds. Later the ships came with steam and electricity and radio.

But the natives were a proud race and soon they changed their opinion of the whites. Instead of thinking of them as gods, they began to think of them as barbarians, whose culture was greatly inferior to their own.

Finally, the British and Americans began to extend their influence in the South Seas, and in 1889 England, Germany, and the United States proclaimed a joint protectorate over Samoa. The plan never worked well, however. Ten years later England withdrew and the United States and Germany divided the group, Germany taking Savaii and Upolu in the west and the United States taking Tutuila in the east. The Germans were mainly interested in trade. The United States wanted a naval base and a coaling station. In the first quarter of the twentieth century the islands of eastern Samoa were ceded to the United States by the high chiefs of the people. Then with the approval of Congress American Samoa became an unincorporated territory. Until 1852 the administration was in the hands of the navy, but for the most part the Samoans were allowed to govern themselves through their churches.

Meanwhile the First World War had ended with the defeat of Germany. Western Samoa was then turned over to New Zealand to govern for the League of Nations and afterwards for the United Nations.

SAMOA FOR THE SAMOANS

More perhaps than any other people in the South Seas the Samoans developed their own distinctive culture. They were not greatly impressed by the civilization that the whites brought. They were not much interested in metal tools and in the many gadgets that the big ships carried. To them life was good because it was easy and simple.

They were good politicians and often had two strong parties. They liked to argue among themselves. Because of this trait they have been called the Irishmen of the Pacific.

It was natural, therefore, that sooner or later they should fight stubbornly for their own independence, though always by peaceful means. On January 1, 1962, Western Samoa won its freedom. The two "high chiefs," or *Fautua*, are now jointly the heads of the state. When one of them dies, the survivor will be the head, and after him the head of the government will be elected by the parliament for a five-year term from among five members of the high chiefs' families.

THE PEOPLE

There used to be many more people in Samoa than there are today, but by 1900 most of them had disappeared. The white man had brought his diseases, you see. Recently, however, there has been a very rapid growth in the population. The latest official figures give almost 114,000. But when you read this there may be 127,000 people on the islands.

The natives are almost all Polynesians with light-brown skin, handsome features, and fine physique. They are brave, intelligent, and honorable.

FA'A SAMOA

The Samoans developed a distinct culture of their own, and they thought this culture was the best possible way of life. They called their customs the *Fa'a Samoa.* They lived like other Polynesians by growing taro, yams, bananas, oranges, and papayas, by collecting coconuts and breadfruit, by fishing and hunting for wild pigs and birds. But in the olden days they still had plenty of time for fighting the people of Fiji and Tonga, and for many ceremonies and happy times among themselves. Their life was described as follows: "Gardening and grove work on Friday, Sabbath preparation on Saturday, church attendance, hymn singing, and visiting on Sunday, recuperation on Monday, fishing, visiting, politicking, and cricket-playing on Tuesday, Wednesday, and Thursday: and then begin again."

They were a contented people and their wants were few and simple. If a man had a good house, a strong canoe, a taro patch with a good fence around it, some coconut and breadfruit trees, and a few pigs, that was enough. They greatly respected their old people, they loved their children, they liked to dance and sing, to play games and visit other villages.

Their houses were round or elliptical and were usually built on a stone platform. The roofs were thatched in the old days. Today some of them are covered with corrugated iron. The roofs are supported by posts set about thirty inches apart, and there are no walls, though there are narrow mats that can be let down in the manner of Venetian blinds.

Most of the villages are on the coast. The interior of the islands is mountainous.

THE MISSIONS

The people had little respect for the whites until the missionaries came. The first of these was John Williams from the London Missionary Society. The missionaries made a deep impression on the natives and the Christian God was immediately adopted by many of the people, though the Samoan ideas and customs were mixed with Christianity. Today more than half of the people belong to London Missionary Society churches.

TUSITALA

The most popular English writer of his day was Robert Louis Stevenson, who wrote *Treasure Island* and many other books. He was born in Scotland in 1850. All his life he struggled with tuberculosis. In his search for health he finally settled on Upolu in Western Samoa, and just outside Apia he built his home. There he spent the last five happy years of his life. The islanders loved him. They called him *Tusitala*, the "Teller of Tales." They built a road to his house, which they called the "Road of the Friendly Heart." There one afternoon in 1894, while gaily tossing a salad for some friends on the porch of his house, he was stricken. That evening he died. The next day sixty stalwart Samoans carried him up a steep little mountain in back of his house and buried him on the top of it.

There on his tomb are carved the lines he himself had written:

> Under the wide and starry sky
> Dig the grave and let me lie.
> Glad did I live and gladly die,
>   And I laid me down with a will.
>
> This be the verse you grave for me:
> *Here he lies where he longed to be;*
> *Home is the sailor, home from the sea,*
>   *And the hunter home from the hill.*

And now the moment has come for us to meet our young Samoan friends. Europa Saipele Le'au is a boy living on American Samoa. Repeka Afioga (pronounced *Ah-fee-ong-ah*) is a girl from a village in the west of Upolu in Western Samoa.

If you were to arrive at the island in a steamer the boys might swim out to greet you with flowers on their heads. And the girls might call out *Ta'alofa!* That means "welcome." Samoa is a very friendly place.

I LIVE IN AMERICAN SAMOA

by Europa Saipele Le'au

MY NAME IS EUROPA

I was named for the continent of Europe but I've never been away from American Samoa. My father is Saipele Le'au Ne'e and he was born in American Samoa too, on the largest island, which is called Tutuila. My mother, however, was born on a smaller island of American Samoa, called Manu'a. She came to Tutuila to work, and my father met her here and married her. I have five sisters and seven brothers. Two of the sisters are married and one of them has two children. The oldest boy is twenty and I am the fifth boy. I was born on my father's plantation fifteen years ago. I call my father *Matai*, which means "master." My mother I call *Tina*, which means "mother."

OUR PLANTATION

My father has a job with the government as a skilled mechanic, so all the boys in the family work on the plantation when they are not in school. We have two acres, and we grow bananas, taro, breadfruit, papayas, coconuts, and vegetables. We sell what we grow in the local market.

Most of the people are like us. They have plantations. But some fish, too, and there are Japanese fishermen who go outside the bay to bring in tuna, which are canned here. Some of the canned tuna is exported.

PAGO PAGO

There are four communities around the bay of Pago Pago. One of them is called Pago Pago, but the most important of them is Fagatogo (pronounced *Fahng-a-tong-o*), and that's where I live. It has about four thousand people living in it.

OUR HOUSE IS MODERN

Our house has one floor and four rooms. It's of wood with a corrugated iron roof, and it has electricity, running water, a toilet, and all the modern conveniences. In a way it's a kind of American house. The old thatched houses of the natives can only be found in American Samoa out in the country.

WHEN I WAS SMALL

I used to play hide and seek with other boys and girls when I was a little fellow. I went fishing in an outrigger canoe also. I used to make shoes out of the halves of coconut shells and tie them to my feet. We usually walk barefoot and it was fun to clatter along with these shoes on, and we often fell down, because it was hard to stand up in them. We made balls out of coconut leaves, and used to pitch round pieces of coconut shell, just as boys in other lands pitch pennies. Then when I was seven I began to play Samoan cricket. This is very exciting and sometimes there are fifty players on each side. The bat is usually just a stick about the size of a baseball bat. The game is not the same as the English cricket.

Of course, I had some work to do also when I was small. My special job was to pick up the leaves that dropped around the house from the breadfruit trees.

ASO *TAMAITI*

This means "Children's Day." Usually the children have to wait on the parents. They do all kinds of little jobs for them. They run the errands and mind the babies and make the fires and light the pipes. They are taught to be very polite to older people. It is bad manners to stand in the presence of adults. We have to sit cross-legged on the floor.

On Children's Day everything is different. Then it is the mothers and fathers who have to wait on us. Everyone goes to church and the children have new clothes, flowers in their hair and around their necks, and new songs to sing. At home there is a party. The children love it, for then the older people serve them first.

SCHOOL

My first school was the elementary school of Fagatogo, where I stayed for six years. For the past three years I have been going to the Poyer School, which is about a mile from my home, and I'm in the ninth grade there. I'm studying English, mathematics, science, government, arithmetic. I've studied agriculture at school too, and I want to be a farmer, but a good one. I like arithmetic and science best.

We all wear a uniform at school. The girls wear blue skirts and white blouses. The boys wear a blue *lava lava* with two white stripes around the bottom of it, and a T-shirt. The *lava lava* is the old Samoan costume which was worn by everyone. It's a wrap-around cloth that fastens at the waist. The boys wear it short, the women wear it long. Of course, in American Samoa many of the men wear trousers and many of the women wear American dresses.

THE SCHOOL DAY

I'm up at six and have bread and milk for breakfast. I walk

to school, which begins at seven forty-five. I take a sandwich with me to eat during the morning and I go home at noon for lunch. From twelve thirty to one I play games outdoors, volleyball, basketball, and cricket. The school has teams, and I'm on the cricket team.

From two to four I work on the plantation at home with my brothers. Then I rest or play before my six o'clock dinner. Our two big meals are much alike. We may have soup, meat or fish, vegetables, bananas, taro, coconuts, and milk. After supper I do some homework and go to bed at nine.

We have no school on Saturday. Then I work on the plantation and go on picnics. My father has a jeep, and we usually find some sandy beach, go swimming, and have a nice lunch.

About once a month I go hunting for wild boars. I usually get one, which my mother cooks.

SUNDAYS

We go to the London Missionary Society Church. We have preaching at eight in the morning and at five in the afternoon. At two thirty we have Sunday School. There are many Catholics on the islands also, and more Mormons than there are Catholics.

LANGUAGES

Of course, everyone speaks Samoan at home, but almost everybody speaks English also. This year I am going over to Avele College in Apia to study agriculture. I'll live in a dormitory there, and after three years I'll get a diploma. In Samoan I might say, *O le ā ou alu a a'oga i Avele ile Tausaga Nei 1963*. That means, "I am going to school at Avele in the year of 1963."

MY HOME IS IN WESTERN SAMOA

by Repeka Afioga

FISHING OFF THE REEF

For fifty years now the girls of my school have been going fishing every Saturday off the reef at Apia. We all wear our school uniform, which is a pink-checked dress with a square collar and off-the-shoulder sleeves. There are about a hundred girls in the school and we all start off at seven o'clock in the morning, marching down the long road to the shore. We carry baskets on poles. It's about two and a half miles each way and the people come out to see us pass. When we get to the reef we have to wade in water, which sometimes comes up to our knees. We go barefoot, as most Samoans do all the time, but the soles of our feet are very tough, and we seldom get cut by the sharp coral.

On the reef we get such things as sea urchins, sea slugs, and baby sharks. We are all very fond of the meat from the baby sharks. At four o'clock we march back to the school again with thirty or forty basketfuls of sea food, which we cover with leaves to protect them from the sun.

THE PAPAUTA GIRLS' SCHOOL

My school is almost seventy years old now. It was founded by a German missionary, when the islands were under the German protectorate. The school is supported by the Congregational and Christian Churches of the islands. It's proud of the fact that its graduates have become many of the Christian mothers of Samoa. Its girls have gone all over the islands of the South Pacific, as missionaries and as the wives of missionaries. They have gone to places like the New Hebrides, the Solomon Islands, and New Guinea.

I have been in this school for two years now, and I'm in form three. This is like the first year of high school. I'm sixteen years old. Before I came here I went to school in my own village, first to the elementary school, which I entered when I was seven, and afterwards to the district school, which is a primary school. Both schools were in my village of Lalomanu in the district of Aleipata at the western end of the island of Upolu.

I'm now studying English, natural science, arithmetic, physics, and social studies (history, geography, government). I'd like to be a teacher when I finish my schooling.

We have two other costumes besides our ordinary pink-checked dresses. On Sunday we dress all in white. We have the same square neck and the initials of our school are on the pockets of our blouses. Then on very special occasions we wear a red sailor collar with white stripes around it.

At the school the girls do most of the work. We keep the buildings clean, mow the big lawns, take care of three cows and a calf, tend the garden, and help with the plantation. Even during our long vacation from December 15 to February 15 some of the girls are always here. We take two weeks at a time to look out for the school and the grounds.

We have church services at the school, and Sunday is an

important day for us. We have a preaching service at eight o'clock in the morning and another at three o'clock in the afternoon. After the morning service we eat and then we have Sunday School from ten thirty to eleven thirty. Then we rest. In the afternoon some of the older girls teach the small children of the neighborhood. Finally there is a Christian Endeavor service in the evening, which is conducted by both the girls and the teachers.

There is an old building on the grounds which the school is going to tear down. Then in its place a chapel will be built in the ancient Samoan style.

A LOVELY SCHOOL

Our school is very beautiful. We have very nice buildings. There are big spreading banyan trees and many flowers. A little farther up the road is the house where Robert Louis Stevenson, the writer, spent his last years. From our school we can see the top of the little mountain where Stevenson's grave lies. Below us the surf of the wide Pacific breaks on the coral reefs.

MY VILLAGE HOME

The village of Lalomanu at the western end of the island is a big village. It has about five hundred people in it. The village lies right on the shore and the mountains rise in back of it. The people live by growing bananas, cocoa, pineapples, taro, breadfruit, and vegetables, and these things they sell in the village market, where every day someone from my family goes to buy food.

The people fish, too, and they think that the bonito is the best fish they catch. My father has an outrigger canoe and he goes fishing about twice a week. I like to go with him when I'm home. I use a little spear which works like a slingshot with a strong rubber band. My father hunts for wild pigs too.

There are no industries in my village, but there are several stores and a church.

MY HOUSE

I have four brothers and four sisters. My oldest sister is married and has five children. My youngest brother is the new baby of the family, six months old. I am the seventh of the children.

There are about thirty people living in a little group of houses built close together. Besides my immediate family there are uncles and aunts, cousins and nephews and nieces. We have four big houses and some smaller ones just for couples.

These houses are typical Samoan houses. We have covered the floor with small round pebbles gathered on the beach. On these pebbles we spread coarse mats made of the leaves of the pandanus plant to sit on. In the evening we lay over two of these coarse mats five or six fine pandanus mats to make a bed. Some of the finer mats have a fringe of gaily colored wool yarn. We use kapok pillows, and if the night is cool we pull a sheet or a cotton blanket up over us. Some of the older people have beds, but most of them prefer to sleep on the floor. We let down mosquito nets at night.

Most of our houses are thatched, but we have one with a corrugated iron roof.

Outside the main house is a small Samoan cooking house. We make a little pit in the floor, light a wood fire in it, and heat some rocks there. Then we cook on the rocks. I often go up on the lower mountainside to gather wood. Our water comes from a tap in the midst of the buildings, and we use oil lamps. The women in the family usually do the cooking and we eat two meals a day, one at nine in the morning and the second at seven in the evening. But, of course, if we get hungry we can have a snack in the middle of the day.

The climate is rather hot in Samoa, but our houses are very cool because the sides are always open, unless we let down the blinds made of coconut palm leaves for privacy or to keep the rain or the high winds out. We get about 250 inches of rain every year in Samoa.

FUN

When I was small I used to take care of the baby, but I had lots of fun too. I used to play *musa*, which is a kind of hopscotch. I love to dance and sing. All Samoans do. I play the ukulele also.

AVA

There is a kind of drink called *kava* in some South Pacific islands. We call it *ava* here, and it's made by pounding the roots of a tree that belongs to the pepper family and mixing it with water. It's seldom used except for important ceremonies. The *ava* is made in a wooden bowl with many legs carved from a tree. It's mixed by a woman who is a kind of village hostess, and is often the daughter of the high chief. She is called the *Taupo*, or the "high girl." When a distinguished visitor comes to the village he is received with speeches and a drink of ava offered to him in a half coconut shell. The guest pours a little of it on the ground. This used to be the offering to the gods. Then he drinks and gives a toast. *Ia manuia*, he says. That means "May you be blessed!"

Samoa is a very religious nation. The motto on its new seal reads, *Fa'avae e le Atua Samoa*. This means "Founded on God is Samoa."

6. NEW ZEALAND

A SOUTH SEAS WONDERLAND

THE BOTTOM OF THE WORLD

New Zealand is the loneliest and at the same time one of the loveliest countries in the world. It's the most out-of-the-way nation on earth. It's 6,000 miles west of Chile, 1,100 miles south of Fiji, 1,200 miles southeast of Australia. There's nothing to the south of it but Antarctica, about 3,500 miles distant. England, its most important market, is some 12,000 miles away. Yet New Zealand is no primitive outpost of civilization. It's one of the most advanced, one of the most cultured countries on the globe.

A CONCENTRATED WONDERLAND

While New Zealand is far away from other nations, it's a little world in itself, and a world of wonders. The Alps of Switzerland are there, their sides scoured by colossal glaciers. The fjords of Norway are there, ten to thirty miles long, and the geysers of Iceland, dozens of them. New Zealand has a mountain cone as perfect as Japanese Fuji. It has lakes as beautiful as those of northern Italy, born of the glaciers, encircled by the mountains. It has beaches like those of the French Riviera. It has fertile farmlands, emerald islands, deep forests, smoking volcanoes, and fair cities.

The highest peak is Mount Cook, 12,349 feet in altitude. The native people of New Zealand, the Maoris, call it *Aorangi*, the "Cloud Piercer," it's so high. But there are a dozen other peaks over ten thousand feet.

Rotorua is one of the most remarkable thermal regions in the world. There are boiling pools where you can see the Maori women cooking their dinner. There are bubbling mud volcanoes, healing mineral waters, crystal-clear springs, unspoiled forests, crater lakes, hot waterfalls, mountains, and steam vents. Some of this steam, which comes bursting out of the earth, has been harnessed to provide electricity and heat.

Another of the marvels of this island wonderland is the Waitomo Caves. There you take a boat on an underground river into a silent grotto, where you look up to a black heaven sparkling with myriads of blue-green lights. These are living jewels, glowworms which transform this dark world into a beautiful, unearthly fairyland. It is doubtful if anywhere else outside of New Zealand you will find another glowworm cavern like this one.

SQUARE MILES AND PLEASANT PEOPLE

New Zealand is composed of two big islands and many small ones. It has a little more than 100,000 square miles, which makes the country just about the same size as Colorado. Italy is a little bigger. The islands are about 1,000 miles long and never more than 280 miles wide. The nation has a population of about 2,300,000. The people are in the main fine and intelligent. About 160,000 of them are Maoris.

VIKINGS OF THE SUNRISE

We have already learned much about these daring navigators that settled in the islands of the Pacific. The Maoris of New Zealand are Polynesians who seem to have come from Tahiti and the Cook Islands. Their principal migration reached New Zealand about 1350 A.D. When they set out in their canoes from their earlier home, one of their prophets said to them, "Go forth to become a great people. Remain at peace one with the other. If you follow the deeds of Tu, the god of war, you will perish as if swept away by the winds."

The canoes in which they traveled were huge hollowed logs, from sixty to eighty feet long. The one that was called the *Tainui Canoe* was pulled up on the shore of their new home six hundred years ago, and left there. It rotted completely away. But the people who arrived in it had placed stones to mark the bow and the stern. These stones were seventy feet apart.

ABEL TASMAN

The islands were discovered on December 13, 1642, by a Dutchman, Abel Tasman, who described them as a "large land uplifted high." Some of the men went ashore and were killed by the natives. So Tasman called the place Murderer's Cove and did not go ashore himself. His report about the islands was naturally not enthusiastic.

However, Tasman will never be forgotten, for the name he gave to the islands he discovered has stuck through all the years. In the south of his native Holland was a district called *Zeeland*, which means the "Sea Land." So he called these islands he discovered Nieuw Zeeland. Everyone now knows them as New Zealand.

Murderer's Cove is now known by the pleasanter name of Golden Bay.

COOK'S GOBLINS

It was more than a century and a quarter later before another white man came to the islands. Others who might have come did not want to meet with the fate of the sailors who landed at Murderer's Cove. But in 1769 our great British navigator and explorer, James Cook, came. He had been sent by the government into the southern seas to find a continent that wasn't there. On the way back he explored the coastland of New Zealand and was the first white man to go ashore after Tasman sailed away. He liked the country and found the people attractive. So he claimed the islands for Great Britain.

When Cook's men rowed ashore the Maoris thought they were goblins. They turned their faces backward as they rowed. They must have eyes in the back of their heads, the natives said. For the Polynesians, as they paddled, always looked ahead. They wanted to see where they were going, as they supposed any sensible navigator would want to do.

THE BRITAIN OF THE SOUTH

Britain wasn't much interested in the islands when Captain Cook visited them. But his favorable report made it certain that sooner or later the white men would come in large numbers. In 1814 missionaries began to enter the country, followed by traders. In 1839 Great Britain signed a treaty with the Maoris by which Queen Victoria became the distant ruler of the land. Then in 1840 white settlers, sponsored by the New Zealand Company, began to come.

In 1907 New Zealand became a dominion in the British Empire. Now she has an important and honored place in the British Commonwealth.

For a time it looked as if the Maoris would disappear. In 1926 there were only about 63,670 of them. But then they began to increase till there were 161,000 in 1960. Today they are moving into the cities and the new industries. They have limited voting rights, but otherwise they have acquired equal privileges.

Most of them are on North Island. You find them at Rotorua and elsewhere. Their houses and meeting places are adorned with fine carvings. They have their ancient music and dances and costumes.

FIVE CITIES

Since 1860 Wellington, at the southern end of North Island, has been the capital of the country. Its motto is *Suprema a situ*, which means "Supreme in her site." The city occupies a big amphitheater on the hills around Port Nicholson Harbour. During the last world war, the whole American South Pacific fleet anchored in this harbor. The population of the city is 220,000.

Auckland, up towards the north of North Island, is the largest city in the country with a population of 391,000. It's one of the world's most important seaports, and like Corinth in Greece it lies between two seas. Hauraki Gulf opens into the Pacific in the east, and Manukau Harbour in the west leads to the Tasman Sea.

Christchurch is the largest city on South Island with 200,000 people. It's located halfway down the east coast. It is sometimes called the Garden City of New Zealand, sometimes the Cathedral City of the Plains. It's a rather young city, having been founded only in 1850. The Avon River flows through it, but the little river with its grassy banks doesn't get its name from the English river Avon, but from a little stream in Lanarkshire, Scotland, which was dear to some of the early settlers.

Down on the southeast coast of the same island stands Dunedin, which is as Scottish as Christchurch is English. It has 100,000 people and is called the Edinburgh of the South.

The fifth of our cities is Queenstown in the south central part of South Island. It's one of the world's most beautiful cities, surrounded on three sides by high mountains and facing on the fourth side Lake Wakatipu, which rises and falls at regular intervals in some strange fashion.

GOLD AND GRASS

Queenstown was the center of a frantic gold rush in the middle of the nineteenth century, when fortunes were made—and lost—almost overnight. But the day of the gold prospector quickly passed. The wealth of New Zealand now comes from other things.

When the first settlers came the country was covered with forests and wild grasses. The settlers laboriously cleared the land and planted it with rich pasture grasses, which were admirably adapted to flocks of sheep and herds of cattle. Today grass has become the gold of New Zealand. Some of the finest sheep country in the world is on North Island. The climate is favorable for sheep raising, with warm summers and mild winters. The seasons are reversed in the Southern Hemisphere. In the middle of January the gardens are abloom everywhere except in the high mountains.

By the way, a flock of sheep is called a mob in New Zealand.

The country is the world's largest exporter of dairy products and lamb, the second-largest exporter of wool. It was the beginning of refrigeration that made it possible for New Zealand to ship meat halfway round the world.

PLEASURE ISLANDS

New Zealand is not only a scenic wonderland. It's also a paradise for sportsmen. Some of the world's best big game fishing is to be enjoyed in the Bay of Islands and other resorts off the northeast coast of North Island. Many of the lakes and streams abound in big trout. It is said that the trout in Lake Taupo on North Island beg to be caught.

For the hunter there are deer, wild pigs, and wild goats, so abundant that they are a pest. The whole year is an open season and no licenses are required. Skiing in the Southern Alps is superb and everywhere there is fine swimming and sailing. To make matters perfect for the visitor there are no land snakes and no wild animals.

Of the two fortunate young people who live in this wonderland Teria Amiria Smiler represents the oldest known inhabitants. She is a Maori girl and lives just outside Wellington on North Island. She is very fond of sports. She tells about herself and her people.

Martin Wyatt Collins is of English descent. He lives in Christchurch on South Island. Like the Maori girl he is very fond of sports.

I AM A MAORI GIRL FROM NORTH ISLAND

by Teria Amiria Smiler

THE LAND OF THE LONG WHITE CLOUD

I am a Maori, and so I should begin by saying *Tena Koe*, which means "How do you do" in my language. In the old days, centuries ago, my people sailed all over the Pacific in their big canoes. No one knows when they first discovered New Zealand, which they called *Aotearoa*, the "land of the long white cloud." But about 1350 there was a great migration here. Some of the people came from Tahiti, which they called Hawaiki, but tradition says my ancestors came from the Cook Islands. The big canoes in which they sailed had names. One of them in the fleet was *Arawa*, and from the people in that canoe came the tribe of Rotorua and Taupo. Another was *Tainui*, and from them came the Waikato people. From *Matatua* came the people of the eastern Bay of Plenty. From *Arotea* came those of the western coast south of Mount Egmont. From *Horouta* and *Takitimu* came the people of the east coast.

Tradition says that my father's ancestors came in the canoe

Takitimu and that the majority of the high priests came in this canoe. So this was one of the most important, if not the most important, of the tribes. Perhaps they left the Cook Islands because there wasn't enough food there. They brought with them to New Zealand seeds and food plants from their old home, but the climate of New Zealand was so much colder than what they had been accustomed to that only the sweet potato lived.

MY FATHER TEACHES THE MAORI LANGUAGE

My father's name is Winiata Kaihote Smiler. He was born in Gisborne, on the east coast of North Island. He now teaches the Maori language at the Wellington Correspondence School. This is a public school, which is mainly intended for country children where there are no convenient schools on the spot. The younger people do not speak our ancient language as much as they used to, and we are trying to keep the old culture alive.

My mother's name is Margaret Wikitoria. She was born in Westport on South Island. This is a coal-mining town. My mother's father was Scottish, but through her mother she is descended from the people of another canoe, the *Arotea.*

MY EARLY LIFE

My name is Teria Amiria Smiler, and I was born fourteen years ago in Wellington, the capital of New Zealand. I was a kind of tomboy when I was small and got into all sorts of mischief. In those years it was very difficult to find a house in Wellington, and we moved five or six times. For a whole year we lived in a transit camp, which was established to help people who could not find houses to live in. You could stay there for six months or twelve months, and each family had a separate place. Finally we moved to Nae Nae, which is about fourteen miles from the center of Wellington, beyond the place they call Lower Hutt. Nae Nae is mainly residential, a commuter town for Wellington, but there is a Phillips Radio factory there.

Our house is a wooden house of one story with six rooms in it.

I am the oldest in my family. There are five others younger than I. My sister Mari is a girl of eleven. She is in standard six. My brother Pera is ten and in standard four, and my brother Kingi is seven and in standard one. There are two more boys, too young to go to school, Enoka and Winiata.

FROM KINDERGARTEN TO COLLEGE

I started in kindergarten when I was about four and entered primary when I was five. Then I went through the intermediate school, and I am now in my first year of college. This is the same as the first year of high school in other places. My college is called Taita College and it is quite close to Nae Nae.

I am now taking Maori by correspondence, and in my college English, French, science, history, art, music, and physical training. We all speak Maori at home, but still I am studying it.

LESSONS AND SPORTS

My day begins at six with chores about the house. The children take turns doing them, making beds, washing dishes, and such things. Then I practice ballet dancing. After that I have breakfast: porridge, sometimes eggs, toast and butter, and milk. School begins at eight thirty. First we have assembly and then classes from nine to ten forty-five. There is a break at ten forty-five and then more classes from eleven to twelve. I eat sandwiches during the lunch hour, and the school supplies milk free. Then we have classes from one to two fifteen, a break until two thirty, and classes again till three thirty.

After that, when it is winter, we play basketball about three times a week. Last year I was the representative of my school in basketball on a kind of all-star team in Nae Nae which plays with other communities.

In the summer we play baseball, and I was on the top baseball team in my school last year. In the late afternoon I often go swimming. In the recent swimming carnival I got first place in the fifty-five-yard race.

I WANT TO BE A BALLET TEACHER

I have private dancing lessons four times a week. We have a competitive society which holds contests in singing, dancing, and things like that. Recently I won the first prize in a ballet contest which they put on. There's a good ballet group in Auckland.

Saturday I have a ballet class and I often go riding on my bicycle with my friends. There are many lovely places to go to, and fine beaches near Wellington, but I don't have much time to swim now.

THE GIRLS BRIGADE

I belong to the Girls Brigade, which is something like the Girl Scouts. It is not run by any particular church. We have many outdoor activities, and we get patches for our uniforms when we have passed certain tests: first aid, country dances, cooking, wood carving, metalworking, and flower growing. Our uniform is a navy-blue, one-piece frock with red trimming. We wear a navy-blue beret also. Our merit patches are worn on a sleeve.

MAORI CUSTOMS AND COSTUMES

There is a Maori Club in Wellington, and, of course, I belong to that. It is trying to keep the old Maori customs alive.

All the different Maori tribes have their own dances and songs, and I know how to do the Maori *poi* (ball) dance. I have a Maori costume. The bodice is of wool woven in a colorful design, and the skirt is of long stalks of flax, which have been cooked, scraped, and dyed, and hang from the waist. Only the parts that have been scraped will take the dye, and different designs in white and black are made on the skirt. I have a headband, too, and my Maori Club has a special design for it.

Around Rotorua in the center of North Island there are many Maoris. They have lived there for generations. They have a model village just like the old fortified *pa.*

TRAVEL

During the long vacation we usually go away for a few weeks. We have often been to Gisborne, for that is my father's birthplace. We have been to Westport too, where my mother was born. Then we have been to other places like Rotorua, Lake Taupo, Chateau, and Hamilton on North Island, and Christchurch and Nelson on South Island.

THE CHURCH OF THE LATTER-DAY SAINTS

My father and all the children go to the Church of the Latter-day Saints. They have a temple in Nae Nae and I attend the morning service, which is for young people. There is a service for adults in the evening but I don't go.

FESTIVALS

In September we have a Blossom Festival at Hastings in the fruit-growing country. Everybody goes. They have a parade of flowers, games, and contests, and they choose a Blossom Festival Queen.

Eastborne, just outside of Wellington, is starting a Mardi

Gras. They will have a baby show, a beauty contest, and swimming races. We already have a harbor swim from one of the islands to one of the beaches, but you have to be sixteen to compete.

I COME FROM SOUTH ISLAND

by Martin Wyatt Collins

MY CITY OF CHRISTCHURCH

I have never been in England but they say my city of Christchurch is the most English city in the world outside of England itself. In the center of it is a lovely church, Canterbury Cathedral, and the whole city is laid out around it. Through the center of the city winds the little river Avon. It has beautiful lawns on each side of it and lovely willow trees. It is another thing that reminds you of England. Many of the public buildings, many of the streets, and many of the ways of the people are just like what you would find in England. And there are many lovely parks here.

My name is Martin Wyatt Collins, and I was born in this city sixteen years ago. Actually I was born in the same house where I now live. This is a single, wooden, one-storied house with seven rooms, about two hundred yards from the Avon, in one of the residential districts of the city.

MY FAMILY

My father's name is Cyrill Wyatt Collins. He works in the Inland Revenue Department. He was born in Lyttleton, only a few miles away, which is the port of Christchurch. He was in the First World War and served in France. Before he got his present job he used to work for a transportation company.

My mother is Yvonne Evelyn. She was born in Christchurch. I have one brother, David John, who is now twenty-three and works in a grain and feed store. He is also in the Naval Reserve and has to give some time to that, mostly in the evening.

MY SCHOOLS

I first went to school at four. This was a kindergarten and I stayed there for one year. Then I went to primary school for five or six years and to intermediate school for two years. I am now in the third year of high school. This is the Christchurch Boys High School. There I am taking French, history, mathematics, English, and physics. I like English best of all, but I haven't made up my mind what I want to do with myself later on.

I get up at seven thirty and my breakfast consists of bread and butter, an egg, and coffee. My school is four miles from my house and I go there on my bike. It takes me about twenty-five minutes. At eight forty we have to be inside for assembly, which is held in the hall. There is a short religious service. Classes last from nine fifteen to three fifteen with lunch from twelve fifteen to one fifteen. I haven't time to go home during that hour, so I bring my lunch to school, always some sandwiches. Sometimes I buy a drink or a sweet.

AFTER SCHOOL

After school we usually have sports practice. We play cricket a great deal. This is a summer game. We have about sixteen school teams and I am on one of them. It is a long game and I am usually playing twice a week. We compete with other schools. In the winter we play football, usually

Rugby, though we play soccer also at school. When I am not playing cricket or football I am playing tennis and golf. If, however, I am not busy with sports in the afternoon I go home, have a cup of tea, and then I do my homework for the rest of the afternoon. Our evening meal, which we call tea, comes about six. We have meat and vegetables, pudding, and coffee. In the winter we usually have soup. At home I help my mother with the dishes and other house chores. When the days are long in the summer I often go out for sports in the evening. But I have to finish my homework then. Sometimes I listen to the radio. I have a dog called Paddy and a cat called Sammy, and since they belong to me I have to feed them in the evening. I am usually in bed by nine thirty.

FRIDAY, SATURDAY, AND SUNDAY

On Friday night we have a Bible class at the church, for I belong to the Church of England. This class is led by one of the older boys.

On Saturday, when we have no school, I spend a good deal of time in our garden helping my father and mother. Almost all the homes in my part of Christchurch have gardens, and we have a nice one. We have nectarines and apples, gooseberries and grapes. We grow enough vegetables for our own use. Saturday afternoon I often play cricket again from about one to five, though I may play football instead. About twice a month I go to the movies on Saturday evening. Other Saturdays I may dance, for the churches often have dances in their parish halls. I play Ping-pong in my parish hall also.

Sunday I go to Communion at nine thirty. My father has a Citroën and I often go visiting with the family. We have friends in Nelson in the north of South Island, and I have been there a couple of times.

I am not fond of indoor games.

VACATION TIME

My long vacation comes from December 12 to February 2. We call these the Christmas holidays. We have also two weeks in May and three weeks in August. During the last Christmas holidays I worked in a fellmongery. You see, Christchurch is in a farming country, the center of wheat growing in New Zealand, and the place where the famous Canterbury lamb comes from. So there are lots of sheep, and in the fellmongery we treat the sheepskins just as they come from the sheep so that the wool comes off very easily. Then we sell the wool and the skins overseas.

I used to do canoeing upstream on the Avon, but I don't do that much now. There are some fine beaches on the sea near the city but I don't like to swim.

In January, 1959, I went to the Scout Jamboree in Auckland on North Island, and had a wonderful time there. I have been in scouting for three or four years now and I am a first-class scout. I have just gone into the Senior Scouts. The scouts have a camp on the Wainakariri River about twelve miles from Christchurch. Sometimes I go there. It's a good place for boating and swimming, but the water comes down from the mountains and it is very cold.

I have been to Queenstown in the south. This is a very beautiful place on the shores of Lake Wakatipu, which is more than fifty miles long. The bottom of the lake is far below sea level, and they say the lake breathes. Every fifteen minutes it rises and falls several inches. There are some jagged mountains back of the lake called the Remarkables, but the really high mountains in what we call the Southern Alps are around Mount Cook. There are some wonderful glaciers there, and it was on these mountains that Sir Edmund Hillary trained for his Mount Everest climb. However, I have never visited Mount Cook.

I haven't been outside of New Zealand yet, but my brother went to the Coronation. He is a Sea Cadet and was chosen to represent them. He also went to Scotland at that time just to see the country.

I speak English and a little French.

There isn't anything very interesting in the way of festivals in my city.

7. FIJI

THE CROSSROADS OF THE PACIFIC

THE BEACH AND THE BUSH

It is time perhaps for us to recognize the difference between what the natives of the South Pacific call the Beach and what they call the Bush. Neither the Beach nor the Bush is a place. Anything that is new or foreign in the Pacific is the Beach. The old way is the Bush. The native magic worker is the Bush. Christ, who was brought to the islands by the missionaries, is the Beach. The Beach is the jeep, the movies, the radio, television, hi-fi, sewing machines, canned salmon, matches, chocolate bars, chewing gum, khaki pants, Coca-Cola, jazz, slang, cigarette lighters, penicillin, gin.

The Bush is the outrigger canoe, rubbing sticks, taboos, tattooing, *poi*, the *lei*, the *luau*, the thatched hut, the hula dances and the war dances, the native dialects, the old gods and goddesses, the ancient legends.

The tourist who travels on the jet planes and the luxury liners sees for the most part the Beach only. This may indeed be the palatial hotels and the surfboards of Waikiki Beach in Honolulu, or it may be the skiing resorts high among the glaciers of New Zealand's Southern Alps. He's not likely to see the old way of life: the men and women whirling about in the public dancing places of the little villages to the accompaniment of big crescent-shaped drums. Or the islanders on some little atoll diving in the deep waters of the lagoons for shells, spearing fish for their dinner, breaking off the husks of the coconuts on a sharpened stake driven into the ground.

CALLING UP THE SEA TURTLES

On Kandavu Island in Fiji the women are able to call the great sea turtles up to the surface of the water. They sing a song about two princesses, who, according to the legend of the country, changed themselves into turtles to escape from their captors. As they sing the turtles appear. But it's said that if there are visitors from a neighboring, rival village, the turtles keep to their hiding places in the depths.

This is the Bush.

FIRE-WALKING

On another little island called Beqa (pronounced *Mbengga*), just off the capital at Suva, the men walk barefoot on a bed of heated rocks without getting their feet burned.

This too is the Bush.

THE FIJI ISLANDS

The international date line, where "tomorrow is yesterday," runs just west of this group of islands in the Southern Hemisphere. There are 322 of them altogether, but many less than half are inhabited. Here are more of the lovely South Sea islands we have been talking about. Most of them are fringed with coral reefs, inside which there are always quiet waters. The largest of the islands is Viti Levu with four thousand square miles. The capital, Suva, has 37,000 people. The second largest island is Vanua Levu with two thousand square miles. On the small island of Ovalau is the former capital of Levuka.

Fiji is the most important group of islands in Oceania north of New Zealand, and Suva is the most important city outside of New Zealand. The location of the islands is so strategic that they have become the travel crossroads for steamers and planes.

THE CANNIBAL ISLANDS

Abel Tasman is usually called the discoverer of these islands in 1642, but there were certain earlier Spanish visitors. Cook came in 1774, Bligh in 1789. The missionaries came in 1835 and helped to abolish cannibalism. For the natives previously had the horrible habit of eating their prisoners. Certain chiefs would eat no meat except what they called "long-pig." When there were no prisoners, they would select a certain family and eat them one by one. The kings put a *tapu* on them, which meant that they were sacred to him. The first missionaries were not Europeans, however, they were Tahitians sent out by the London Missionary Society.

Before the missionaries arrived the traders began to come to get the sandalwood, which was very fragrant, and so in great demand.

For many years after Bligh came the islands were called the Bligh Islands. You can still see in the Suva museum the rudder of Bligh's ill-fated ship. The *Bounty* was burned and sunk at Pitcairn Island by the mutineers who went there. Many years afterward, in 1932, the wreck was discovered and raised. The British government sent the rudder to Suva. It was not far away that the mutiny took place.

The native name for the islands is Viti. Most of the earliest ships, however, arrived by way of Tonga, where the islands were known as Fichi. The Europeans called them Feejee, and Fiji they have remained to this day.

Since 1874 Fiji has been a British Crown colony, the most important British colony in the Pacific.

Some of the descendants of the old cannibals may be found now singing in the church choirs of Suva.

THE MELANESIANS

We have been talking about the Polynesians in our previous chapters. Here we have for the first time the Melanesians. Long before Abel Tasman or any of the other Europeans arrived the Melanesians came from East Asia. They may have been the first great migration to venture out from Indonesia into the Pacific. They probably settled in New Guinea, the Solomon Islands, the New Hebrides, and New Caledonia before they arrived in Fiji. Their skin was darker than that of the Polynesians and they had thick, crinkly hair. There are about 148,000 of them in the islands today.

OTHER RACES

The development of the sugar and pineapple plantations led to the importation of Indians from southern Asia. They were indentured, that is, they were bound by contract to work for their masters on these plantations. In a couple of years there were 2,000 of them, and the Indian population has grown so rapidly during the succeeding years that they now outnumber the Melanesians. There are almost 170,000 of them today. Most of them are Hindus in their religion, but about ten per cent of them are Moslems.

Besides the two main groups there are about 6,500 Europeans and about 4,000 Chinese. The total population is about 328,000.

FIJI FESTIVALS

A Fiji *meke*, or "feast," accompanied by singing and dancing, is delightful. There are no dishes, no cutlery. The plates are leaves, or sea shells, or cocount shells, and you eat with your fingers. There are many different kinds of food: crab, crayfish, shellfish, *dalo* (which is the taro of Hawaii), *kokoda* (which is "pickled fish"), and all kinds of tropical fruits. If you were a guest at such a meke, you would sit on pandanus mats laid on the ground.

For the Hindus the "Festival of Lights," which they call *Dewali,* is just as important as Christmas is for Christians. It comes toward the end of October and celebrates the victory of good over evil. There are lights everywhere, candles and oil lamps in the windows, strings of electric lights along the balconies and down the steps, bonfires, and firecrackers.

But when we speak of firecrackers we think first of all of the Chinese in Fiji and their New Year's celebration. This festival sometimes lasts for as much as fifteen days, and on New Year's Eve there is a loud popping everywhere when the Chinese light their long strings of firecrackers. This is the time when everyone tries to pay his debts, when the children find "lucky money" wrapped in red paper under their pillows, and when the families sit down together for big dinners. The Chinese give fanciful names to their food then. Eggs are "silver bars," mushroom are "opportunities," taro is "good fortune," vegetables are "Buddhist scepters."

Fiji is a beautiful and a happy place to visit. Viti Levu is indeed rapidly becoming the Beach for the many tourists who now arrive, but most of the little islands are still the unspoiled Bush for the simple Melanesians who live there.

Nanise Waga is a Melanesian girl who goes to a fine boarding school, but she tells us many things about her life at home and on her father's farm. Ramesh Chandra is an Indian boy, whose father is a tailor. These two young people from the crossroads of the Pacific would like us to visit their lovely islands. If we did, they would greet us with the words, "Bula-Welcome."

I AM A FIJI GIRL

by Nanise Waga

THE FIJI LANGUAGE

In my language we pronounce some of the letters in a very special way. The *d* sounds like *nd*, the *b* like *mb*. The *c* sounds like *th*. The *g* like *ng*. The *q* like *ngg* in *finger*. The name of my school is Adi Cakobau. But it is pronounced *Andi Thakombau.*

NADI AND SUVA

I was born fifteen years ago near Nadi (pronounced *Nandi*), which is the most important place in the western part of Fiji. All the big airlines touch there. But the place where I was born was a little fishing village right on the shore called Delaiyadua. I lived there until I was ten and started my schooling there when I was six. This was in the district primary school.

Now I live about ten miles from Suva, which is the capital of Fiji near the southeastern corner of Viti Levu. When we first moved here we lived in a house near my school, where my father, whose name is Taraiasi, was a cook. My father isn't a cook there any more. He is now a farmer and he grows taro, yams, bananas, cassava, cucumbers, oranges, lemons, and melons. Some of these things he sells, and the family eats the rest.

A FIJI HOUSE

When my father gave up his job as a cook at the school we moved to another house a little farther away. This is a rectangular house with thatched walls and a high-peaked thatched roof. There is a door at one end, and two more doors in the middle of the long sides. Inside there is just one big room where all nine of us sleep. My father has a bed to sleep on, but the rest of us sleep on mats on the floor.

This is not as uncomfortable as it sounds, for this is the way we lay our floors. First we cover the ground with bamboo. Then we place over the bamboo a thick layer of ferns, which we change every few weeks. Then we lay overlapping mats on top, and on them our old rugs of straw or raffia. Finally we lay our best big rugs on top of everything. You see it's quite soft to sleep on.

We have no table or chairs, but we do have low stools. Outside the house there is a separate kitchen for cooking. We have a big round iron pot there filled with small stones. On top of the stones a wood fire is built until the stones are very hot. The food, which has been wrapped in leaves, is then placed on the stones, and sometimes the whole is covered with earth. If we are cooking a pig we fill the body with hot stones so that the meat will be cooked through.

There is no electricity in our house and we get our water from a nearby stream.

My father has some hens, one cow, and a bullock. The bullock, however, is still too small to use. We have three dogs and one cat.

My mother's name is Temalesi. The oldest of the children is Meli. He is a boy of nineteen and he goes to a general college near Suva. He wants to be a teacher. After him comes my sister Veniana, who is seventeen. She goes to my school. Then I come, and all the younger children are boys. There is Kolinio, who is twelve and goes to a Methodist school for boys and girls at Davuilevu, not far away; Taraiasi, a boy of ten, who is at the village school of Sawani; Anasa, a boy of six, at the same village school; and Taniela, a boy of three, who, of course, is still too young to go to school at all.

A MODERN GOVERNMENT SCHOOL

My school is a wonderful government school for girls. We have about 190 girls who are all boarders. I am a boarder too, and I am now in form three. The school is at Sawani and is a modern school with beautiful buildings and a large plantation around it. There are primary, intermediate, and secondary courses. The school has many different kinds of tropical trees growing on the grounds, and there are large plantings of mahogany trees, coffee trees, and banana plants. There are also many cows and hens and a big farm for vegetables.

I have English, the Fiji language, geography, history, and natural science. I like the last subject best, and I want to be a teacher.

MY DAILY ROUTINE

I get up at six and then I spend an hour cleaning the classrooms and the grounds. At seven thirty I have bread, fruit, and milk. After breakfast I help to clean up the dormitories. Some of the big dormitories have beds for sixteen girls. I sleep in one of the smaller ones where there are beds for only ten girls.

We all wear a uniform, which consists of a red skirt with white blouse and collar. The uniform has red buttons and on the left side of the blouse we wear the school emblem. After we have cleaned our dormitories we have parade with inspection by the prefects. There are twelve of them. This is followed by a little service of worship with Bible readings and prayers by the principal. We sing hymns too.

Our classes begin at eight thirty and last until eleven thirty. Then we have lunch in the school dining hall. Taro is the staple food for us, but we have other vegetables also. We sometimes have watermelon and pineapple. There are more classes from one fifteen to three thirty, when we all go to work on the school farm where we take care of the vegetables and the fruit trees. We are always setting out new fruit trees too. We only work for an hour, from three thirty to four thirty, and then we have sports for another hour, basketball, volleyball, hockey, and softball. I like these games very much. At five thirty I clean up and we have dinner from seven fifteen to eight fifteen, when we go to bed. The seniors, however, study until nine.

THE WEEKEND

There is no school on Saturday. Then we wash our clothes and clean up the compound. We may wash our clothes any day, if we want to, instead of going to sports. After lunch on Saturday we are free until three forty but I usually stay in the dormitory and read. In the latter part of the afternoon we have sports and in the evening we have shows and dances, to which we may invite the boys.

On Sunday I go to the Methodist church in the town, where we have a service at nine thirty. The preacher comes from another town and the sermon is usually in Fiji, though he sometimes speaks in English. After service we are free until lunch but we must stay on the school grounds. I usually write letters after lunch and we may have visitors from two thirty to four thirty. At five we have hymn practice.

We have a radio at the school, and there are different school clubs. I belong to the senior dramatic club, which meets after school on Wednesdays. The club gives plays about twice a term.

BETTER WAYS OF LIVING

My school is trying to teach the people better ways of living. There is a model hut on the grounds which is like our native houses, but also has a number of improvements. There is a zinc-covered kitchen table, shelves for the food, and a screened box to keep the ants out. There is also a wardrobe for clothes, and a veranda where the man can sit and smoke away from the room where the people sleep. These things are not common in our huts.

THE LONG VACATION

Our long vacation runs from the beginning of December to about February 8. Then I am home with my family. I help my mother with the housework and my father on the farm. We have a radio at home that I listen to, and we play cards a good deal. On Saturday, while I am home, I usually go to the movies. I like to go fishing with a rod and line. Only the boys do spear fishing. I swim and dive in a river near my home, and I have been out to the coral reefs in a boat.

FIJI FEASTS

We have many feasts on Fiji. The people hunt for wild pigs and if they get one they have a big feast. Of course, when we marry we have a big feast too, and when there are distinguished visitors there is another big feast. When visitors come we give them a *tabua*, or "whale's tooth," in a ceremony of welcome. This is also given to a girl when she gets married.

YAGONA

We have a special kind of drink called *yagona*. In other places in the Pacific it is often called *kava*. The drink is made from the root of the pepper plant, which is pounded into a wet mass, mixed with water, and strained. It is not intoxicating, and is a kind of ceremonial drink. When a new governor arrives on the island it is given to him. When a new chief is installed he gets a drink of it. And when an important visitor comes a bowl of it is offered to him.

AN INDIAN BOY IN FIJI

by Ramesh Chandra

THE THREE-LEGGED STOOL

I live on our largest island, which is called Viti Levu. The name means simply "Big Fiji." There are three important races on the island, the Fiji, the European, and the Indian. They have been called the three-legged stool on which the government rests. I am an Indian boy. I was born in Suva, the capital, fifteen years ago.

I WENT TO SCHOOL IN INDIA

My name is Ramesh Chandra. You can write it as a single word, if you like. I do not have a family name. I lived in Suva for three years and then my father took me back to India to visit my family. I stayed with them in Bombay Province for four and a half years before I came back to Fiji.

It was while I was in India that I first went to school. I was six then, and for one and a half years I attended the primary school called Navsari. The place was partly farming and partly industrial. We were living then with my grandparents. The town was not on a river, nor among the hills. It was on the plain.

MY FATHER IS A TAILOR

My father's name is Jamnades. He was born in India in this little town of Navsari. Then his father brought him to Fiji. He was eleven then. His grandfather urged him to come. So he did and he became a tailor. He now has a shop in the center of Suva.

My mother is Rewaben, and she was born in Navsari too. I have one brother and three sisters. The oldest of us is Chandrakant. He is a boy of twenty-one. Chandrakant is his first name. If he wants to he can add his father's name and this is often done. He is not married and is a clerk. Next comes a sister who is married. Her name is Mrs. Pushpa Kapadia. Pushpa is her first name and Kapadia is her husband's name. Her husband is an accountant. They have no children.

Lilawati is a girl of seventeen and Pramila a girl of sixteen. They both help my mother at home with the housework.

MY SCHOOL IN SUVA

When I was seven and a half I came back from India, and I am now in form three of the Marist Brothers High School. This is a private school and my family has to pay for me. Form three is the first year of the secondary school.

I am studying Latin, French, English, physics, chemistry, geometry, algebra, mathematics, history, and sports. I like all these subjects, and I haven't yet decided what I want to be later.

THIS IS MY DAY

My day begins at five thirty or six and I usually read a story book after I get up until breakfast time at seven thirty. Then I have bread and butter, milk or tea. Sometimes I have an egg too. Then I go to school. My school is about two miles from my house in the center of the city and I go there in a bus.

The school day is from eight forty to three and we have an hour for lunch at twelve thirty. I usually take sandwiches from home, and I buy ice cream or cake or chocolate or a coke. About twice a week we have sports in the latter part of the morning. Our school team plays other schools.

I go home at three, and then I usually play cards for a while with my sister or my friends. I like chess and checkers and Monopoly. After I have played for a time I study for an hour and a half and then I take a bath and have my dinner. I am fond of *roti*, which is a "round, flat bread made out of wheat." We eat it with rice and curry. There is a kind of curry called *dhal* which we like very much. Then we have "mustard pickles," which we call *chutney*. We eat fruit and sometimes sweets, and we drink water. After dinner I rest a while or listen to the radio. Then I do homework until nine thirty or ten, when I go to bed.

SATURDAY ACTIVITIES

We have no school on Saturday. At six in the morning I usually go shopping at the market for my family. I don't have to bargain much, for the prices are usually fixed. When I come home I have my breakfast, and then I go to the tailoring shop to help my father. I sell shirts and other things.

I used to go to a radio show that came every Saturday. It was a quiz show and was called *Aap kitna jante hain*, which is Hindustani for "How much do you know?" They asked the boys and girls questions on history and geography. I won several prizes when I took part in it, a fountain pen and some other things. And I didn't cheat.

In the afternoon I go to the Carnegie Library to get books. I like adventure tales, science fiction, detective stories, and cowboy stories. I also go swimming and take walks with my

friends. I swim in the city. About twice a month I go to

the movies. We have a good many Hindustani pictures, most of them made in Bombay, but I see American films also.

My father has a car, but he doesn't drive himself. However, my uncle and my brother drive and on Sundays we often take short drives out of the city. Then I read a great deal and play games and do some homework.

I have been to the island of Mukulau in a small boat. There is a fine beach there. I have also been in a small launch to the island of Ovalau.

When I came back from Bombay I took a boat to Sydney in Australia, then the Pan American plane to Nadi and finally a bus to Suva.

I AM A HINDU

I am a Hindu in religion and there is a Hindu temple here. I seldom go there on Sundays but I do go on the special religious holidays.

FESTIVALS

We have a beautiful Hibiscus Festival in October. We have many games in the park, including gambling games. We have parades with floats and dances at the Grand Pacific Hotel. There are two special events. One of them is the Fiji *mekes*, or "feasts." The other is the Hindu cultural dances. We celebrate this festival for eight or nine days. We choose a Miss Hibiscus then too.

Cession Day on October 10 is also important. This reminds us of the time when the chiefs, meeting in the old capital of Levuka, ceded the island to New Zealand. This is a day for speeches and parades. It is being suggested now that Cession Day should be made a part of the Hibiscus Festival, but many people don't like the idea.

PEN PALS

I now have four pen pals, one in Malaya, and three in New Zealand. I speak English, Gujarati, and Hindustani. These last two languages are Indian. In Gujarati we say *Kem chhe* for "How do you do"; in Hindustani we say *Kaise hey*.

8. NEW CALEDONIA

THE FERTILE CRESCENT

THE FERTILE CRESCENT

The stepping stones over which the Melanesians passed on their way to Fiji were the big island of New Guinea, the Bismarck Archipelago, the Solomon Islands, the New Hebrides, and New Caledonia. If you look on your map you will see that they form a crescent which with the continent of Australia encloses the Coral Sea. These islands are sometimes called the Fertile Crescent. That's an apt name for them too, for they are very rich in minerals and foods.

In comparison with its size New Caledonia, for instance, has the richest mineral resources in the world. Next to Canada it's the world's most important source of nickel. It has twenty million tons of iron ore. It has large deposits of chromite, which is used in making chrome steel and other alloys. It has copper, lead, platinum, gold, and cobalt. The last of these is another important metal in the making of certain kinds of steel.

The name "cobalt" has a very interesting history. When the ore was first discovered and the early chemists melted it, they found to their surprise that it did not give them the metals they expected to get. People, therefore, said that this must be the work of a mischievous goblin. The German word for "goblin" is *Kobold*, and that is what the ore is now called.

Some of the ore in New Caledonia is very easy to mine. Most of the nickel is on the surface. The cobalt, however, is underground.

All these metals were very important during the Second World War, and it was very fortunate indeed that the islanders threw in their lot with Free France and General Charles De Gaulle. Some of our American soldiers were stationed on the island then.

New Caledonia is rich in foodstuffs also. Coffee is the most important crop, but copra, manioc, corn, wheat, and fruit are also grown and exported, as well as tobacco and cotton.

How fertile the country is may be seen from the fact that there are two thousand species of plants, three-fourths of which are found nowhere else on the globe, except a few as fossils.

THE CALEDONIAN CIGAR

On the map the country looks like a long cigar floating on the sea from northwest to southeast. It's about 250 miles long and 30 wide. It's about the size of Connecticut and Rhode Island combined, a total of 6,300 square miles. It lies about 700 miles east of Australia and 900 miles north of New Zealand.

Like many others of these South Sea islands New Caledonia is a dream of beauty. Down the center of it runs a range of mountains that rise to about five thousand feet. The range opens at each end to form a big V.

The eastern side of the island is the windward side. It gets plenty of rain and is typically Polynesian in appearance. It has dense forests, red plateaus, high cliffs, waterfalls, and little villages strung along the coast. There are many small rivers that rush down from the tangled mountains of the interior. Coconut palms fringe the beaches, tree ferns are sometimes 60 feet high, and the araucarian pine towers 150 feet into the air with a tiny tuft of branches at the top that makes it look like a feather duster.

THE CORAL REEF

From one to ten miles off the western shore and parallel with it runs a long coral reef, leaving a quiet, navigable channel between it and the coast. Opposite the mouths of the many short streams there are gaps in the reef through which ships can enter. The deep blue of the outer ocean is separated from the pale green-blue of the lagoons by the white foamy lace of the waves breaking on the reef.

THE LOYALTY ISLANDS

New Caledonia has dependencies. The most important are the Loyalty Islands, but there are a number of others. The nearest of these outer islands and one of the loveliest is the Isle of Pines. It lies right in the middle of the reefs. From the plane that carries you there you look down into a painter's paradise of brilliant hues. The little island is unbelievably beautiful.

THE GOVERNMENT

All these islands make up one of the overseas territories of the Republic of France. The governor is also the French High Commissioner in the Pacific and the French Commissioner of the New Hebrides. The capital of the territory is Noumea on the southwest corner of the island. This tin-roofed capital is the only large port.

THE PEOPLE

New Caledonia plus its dependencies covers a total area of about 7,700 square miles, and the total population is about 65,000. About 20,000 of these are French, about 30,000 are natives, who are called *kanakas*, and about 12,000 are Tonkinese from Vietnam and Javanese from Indonesia.

THE HISTORY OF THE ISLANDS

Here comes once more that great English explorer, Captain James Cook. It was he who discovered New Caledonia in 1774. The mountains on the island reminded him of Scotland, so he named the place New Caledonia. *Caledonia* was the old Latin name for Scotland. But Cook remained only long enough for his astronomers to watch an eclipse of the sun.

The early history of the islands after Cook sailed away was not very pleasant. Seamen who had deserted their ships came, runaway convicts, and fortune seekers. The natives, too, were very fierce. Perhaps they had to be to deal with this kind of immigrant. But after the crew of a French ship had been killed and eaten by them, the French government stepped in in 1853.

Then in 1864 France established a prison colony there. Still there was trouble with the natives. The last serious incident was the attack upon a white settlement by a chief named Noel. Some of his victims were eaten. Then at last France adopted severe measures, and since then there has been little trouble.

Some of the convicts were employed in the mines, but there was no good labor supply on the island. So workers were imported from southeast Asia. In later years hundreds of Japanese came as miners.

THE LIFE OF THE PEOPLE

The waters around New Caledonia are what the French call a *mer poissonneuse*, a "fish-filled sea." So the people depend a good deal on the ocean for their food. They have a clever way of catching the spiny lobsters that lurk in the coral reefs. They tie a dead squid to a pole and wave it in front of the lobsters. This terrifies them so that the divers can easily seize them.

The interior of the island is full of deer and half-wild cattle. The deer used to be pests, as they still are in New Zealand. But there's a good market for their skins now in Australia.

Once or twice a year the semi-wild cattle are rounded up by the stockmen. They call it a *travail au calicot*, a "calico job." And that's just what it is. The horsemen take a long stretch of cotton cloth. It's half a mile long and a yard wide. With this long strip of cloth they herd the frightened animals into an enclosure where there are tame cattle. The wild ones are afraid to break through the flimsy white band.

Then they are left there without food or water for five days, after which they are quite ready to follow the tame beasts down to the valley pastures that lead to the coast.

The national bird of New Caledonia is the *kagu*. It's like the New Zealand *kiwi* in that it can't fly. It barks like a dog. It's rare now, for it finds it very difficult to escape from the hunters and their dogs by running.

Félix Vakie is a Melanesian boy living on the Isle of Pines the simple life of an island native. Annie Grebe is a French girl from Noumea who was born in Germany after the Second World War. Her father was a French soldier stationed there. After a few months the family moved back to France, where she lived until she was ten. She says that in one way she's typical of the French people who go to New Caledonia, stay for a few years, and then go back to France again.

I AM A MELANESIAN BOY

by Félix Vakie

THE *ÎLE DES PINS*

I was born thirteen years ago at St. Philippe in the Village Vao on the Île des Pins (The Isle of Pines), a very small island that lies in the ocean off the port of Noumea. I don't know the month or the day, and my parents don't remember. I still live in the house where I was born, and my father was born there before me. We have always lived here.

MY FATHER IS A FARMER AND A SHOPKEEPER

My father's name is John Vakie. He is a farmer and a shopkeeper. He grows taro, yams, potatoes, and coconuts. He exports some food, mostly potatoes. When he has some food to sell he goes by a native boat to Noumea. My father also runs a little shop where he sells the food, clothing, and other things the natives need. There are about four shops like this on the island.

My mother's name is Madeleine, and she, too, was born on the island. There are five boys and four girls. The oldest of the children is a girl of sixteen. Her name is Marie du Rosaire. The next is a boy of fourteen, named Josef. Then

I come. The youngest of us all is Bernadette, who is only a year old. These names were all given to us by the church, but we all have native names also.

THE CATHOLIC MISSION SCHOOL

All of us except the very youngest go to the Catholic Mission School. The mission was one of the first missions to be established on these islands. It was started in 1848. It is run by the Marist Fathers and is called the Mission of Vao.

I began school when I was seven. I entered the primary class. Now I am in the first class, which is the highest in the primary school. Next year I'll be in what we call the second year of the middle school, which is the lowest class in the intermediate. When I get to be sixteen I will take my *certificat d'études*.

I am taking geography, history, French literature and grammar, music, and religion. I like history best of all, and later I want to go to Noumea and study to be a Catholic brother.

I LIVE AT THE SCHOOL

I live at my school and get up every morning at four. Then I get ready for church, and we have Mass at four thirty. At five we have our breakfast, which is bread and tea. Then come classes from seven to ten. At ten we go to the fields to work. These are the mission fields, of course, and they grow the same vegetables my father and the other islanders grow. I am in the fields until twelve and I work very hard. Then at twelve we have lunch, sometimes meat or fish. We always have fruit and bread. We drink tea.

After lunch we boys amuse ourselves until two thirty. I usually play football. We have one more class from two thirty until three, when we get a snack to eat. Then we return to the fields until five. After that we go back for dinner. But this time our families bring the food and we eat it outdoors.

The island is small and our houses are seldom very far from the school. We usually have fish and yams. Then there is a half hour of prayer at the church. We study until it is dark and are in bed by seven thirty.

All the boys sleep in one big room and there are three brothers that sleep with us. There are 110 boys at the school. At the other end of the town there is another school for the girls.

Our program on Saturday is exactly the same as on the other days.

On Sundays we stay at the school until after the nine-thirty Mass. I sing in the choir. After church I go home for the rest of the day, returning only in the evening when it is time to be at the mission.

OTHER ACTIVITIES

During vacation I am home with my family and I work in the fields for my father. I like to fish too. My father has an outrigger canoe and I often go fishing with a "spear," which is called a *sagaie*. I go turtle fishing also. To catch a turtle you have to jump on it and turn it over.

I have a dog called *Matelot*. In French that means "sailor."

I have been to the capital of New Caledonia, Noumea, a number of times, but I don't like it there. I'd rather be on my own little island.

WHEN VISITORS COME

Whenever a visitor comes we have native dances and feasts. If the visitor is important there is a dinner at the big chief's house. Then the people come to entertain him with singing and dancing. Even on our small island we have different tribes and every tribe has its own dialect and its own dances. The dances are often historical. They tell of the time when the French came and took possession of the island. They tell of the old days when one island fought with another. Some of the dances represent the ghosts, for the people still believe in ghosts or spirits. During these festivals the people dress in the old costumes. They wear coconut leaves that hang from the waist, and big straw hats decorated with shells.

The men are the only ones that dance. The women accompany them with singing.

We are always glad when important people come, for we have a very good time entertaining them.

THE CORAL REEFS

The Isle of Pines is right in the midst of the coral reefs, and we think it is very beautiful. There is a lagoon in the middle of the island where the water is a lovely light blue and green and other colors. There are wonderful white sandy beaches and big trees. We have some large caves too, and everywhere orchids and other flowers grow.

Our island is so beautiful that they have built a little inn here with a central eating and lounging place and separate little bungalows under the *buni* trees. They have a tennis court and horses you can ride. People come here by air, for there is an airfield in the center of the island, and a plane flies in from Noumea several times a week.

The only languages I know are my native Melanesian dialect and French.

I AM A FRENCH GIRL IN NEW CALEDONIA

by Annie Grebe

MY FAMILY KEPT MOVING AROUND

My name is Annie Grebe and I was born thirteen years ago at Freiburg in Breisgau, Germany. After the Second World War my father was in the French army, and the family kept moving around. We stayed in Freiburg for only two or three months after I was born, and then we went to Bort-les-Orgues in the department of Corrèze, France. I was five when we moved away from that place to Neuvic d'Ussel in Corrèze, and there we stayed for another five years. Then we came to New Caledonia.

I suppose I'm not a typical New Caledonian girl because I've only been here for a few years. But at least I'm typical of the French people here, for many of them come for a few years and then go back to France again.

My father's name is Albert Grebe. He is now working for a private mining company.

My mother's name is Gilberte Donnadieu. She works in a store. Both my parents were born in France.

I have one brother who is older than I. He is twenty and he, too, was born in France. He is now studying in the hospital here, which is called the Hôpital Gaston Bouret. When he finishes at this school he will go to France to study at Bordeaux in the naval hospital, called the Santé Navale. He will remain there for four years.

MY PRESENT SCHOOL IS AT NOUMEA

When I was five I began my schooling at the primary school of Neuvic d'Ussel, and I continued in school there until we came here. I am now in the fourth form of the Collège la Pérouse at Noumea, which is the capital of New Caledonia. I am studying French, English, German, algebra, natural science, geography, history, music, art, gymnastics, and sewing. I like my English and natural science best and I should like to be a teacher, perhaps a teacher of English.

We live in one of the suburbs of Noumea. Our house is a single house of concrete. It has five rooms, all on one floor.

PROGRAM FOR THE DAY

I get up at six and have a continental breakfast. This is usually coffee and milk and rolls. My father drives me to school every morning. We have a Citroën two-hundred horsepower car and it takes only five minutes. Classes begin at seven fifty and last until eleven fifteen. After each class we have a five-minute interval.

At noon I go home in a school bus and have my lunch at eleven forty-five. This is always meat or fish, vegetables and salad, cheese and fruit. I drink water. My father comes home for lunch, and then he drives me back to school for the afternoon session, which lasts from one thirty to four thirty. After that I come home for bread and tea and cakes. Then I sit down to do my homework until dinner time at seven thirty. We usually have soup for dinner, but otherwise it is very much the same as lunch. After dinner I study again for a little while, but I also play the violin and listen to the radio. I am in bed by nine or nine thirty.

We have gymnastics for two hours every week. I play basketball. At home I also play checkers and chess and cards.

We have school on Saturday morning. In the afternoon I help my mother with the wash and study some more. Once in a while I go to the movies.

SUNDAY WORSHIP AND PICNICS

I belong to the Catholic church and on Sunday morning I go to Mass in the Église St. Jean Baptiste. Often on Sunday afternoon the family goes off for a picnic. There are many beautiful places to go to on New Caledonia, but we usually don't go very far. We go to some nice place on the shore or by one of the rivers. Near the city is a very beautiful beach called Anse Vata and we love to go there. Nearby is a wonderful aquarium, where you can see the various kinds of corals and sea anemones and fishes that live 150 feet beneath the surface on the reefs. The corals there are not dead corals. They are just as alive as the fish.

TRAVELS

I have traveled all over New Caledonia. But, except for these travels and my early wanderings in Europe, the only long journey I have ever made was in the steamer of the French line Messageries Maritimes that brought me here. We boarded the ship at Marseilles in southern France, sailed across the Mediterranean to Algiers, then through the Strait of Gibraltar to Madeira in the Atlantic, then over the Atlantic Ocean and through the Panama Canal, across the Pacific Ocean to Tahiti, then to Sydney, the capital of Australia, then to the New Hebrides, and finally to Noumea. It was a long journey and very interesting.

HOLIDAYS

All over the French world the people celebrate the fourteenth of July, the anniversary of the day when the great fortress in Paris, called the Bastille, was captured. Here in Noumea, in addition to the parades and fireworks, we have also yacht races and fishing contests to see who can catch the largest fish.

For us in New Caledonia the twenty-fourth of September is also important. This is the anniversary of the day when the French took over the island of New Caledonia. But we have introduced our own special customs into the celebration. This is the day when we choose a queen of the island. She must be born here, so I could never be chosen queen. While most of the people are Melanesians and dark-skinned, the queen is always white. There is no rule about this. It is just the custom.

At *Noël,* or Christmas, we have one special custom that is interesting. *Père Noël,* or "Father Christmas," always arrives in a boat at the Quai des Militaires. This is the army wharf.

At New Year's we have balls and feasts.

I like the climate here very much. We are in the tropical zone, but the trade winds cool us off.

I have a dog named Ploum and a cat named Coquin.

I speak French and some English.

9. GUAM

THE UNITED STATES IN THE WEST PACIFIC

MICRONESIA

We come now at last to the third great division among the Pacific Islands. This is Micronesia, the little islands. There are very many of them, and they fall into several different groups. The largest group is the Caroline Islands, which were named for King Charles II of Spain. East of the Carolines are the Marshall Islands, and southeast are the Gilbert Islands. These two groups were named for the British captains who explored them. North of the Carolines are the Marianas, which used to be called the Ladrones.

All of these islands together cover only about two thousand square miles. That's the size of Delaware. But they spread over an expanse of ocean as big as the whole United States. Some of these islands have been very important. Guam in the Marianas and Yap in the Carolines used to be vital as land stations for our cable lines. Truk in the Carolines was a great Japanese naval center and their key to the South Pacific. The

Spanish galleons sailing from Acapulco in western Mexico to Manila in the Philippines used to stop at Guam. Bikini and Eniwetok in the Marshalls have been very valuable for our nuclear bomb testing.

Micronesia is entirely in the tropics. The people who migrated there were light-colored sea wanderers from the southwest.

THE ISLANDS OF THIEVES

On March 6, 1521, Ferdinand Magellan, the Portuguese navigator sailing under the Spanish flag, reached some inhabited islands in the West Pacific. The watch in the main top saw a mountain peak in the distance and with tears running down his face and with his voice cracking with emotion he cried out: "Praise God! Praise God! Land! Land! Land! Land!"

It was the island we now call Guam. And no port on any sea has ever been greeted with louder shouts of joy. For these men the passage across the Pacific had been an awful ordeal. Many of the sailors had died of scurvy. Their food and water were exhausted. They had eaten the shipboard rats, the leather that covered the mainyard, the greasy sawdust scraped from the inside of the empty pork barrel. The crew was too weak to lower the heavy sails. They cut the halyards with their axes. Then they shoved the skiff overboard, but before the landing party could man it many outrigger canoes with lateen sails came dashing out from the shore. The natives swarmed over the sides of the vessels and immediately began to steal everything on board that was not nailed down. Hatchets, pails, knives, and every other metal object particularly tempted them. Finally Magellan was compelled to order his men to shoot with their crossbows. The natives fled but they took the skiff with them.

The next day Magellan bombarded the village and sent a landing party ashore. The half-starved men gathered up all the pigs and chickens, all the coconuts, yams, bananas, and breadfruit they could find and filled their empty casks with water. On a neighboring island they got more provisions by barter. Then the ships sailed away. Shortly after they reached the Philippines, where Magellan was killed in a fight with the natives. One of his vessels, the *Victoria*, sailed on around the Cape of Good Hope and was the first ship to circumnavigate the globe.

THE NAMES OF THE ISLANDS

Magellan called Guam and the neighboring islands the Ladrones. That means "thieves" in Spanish. It's easy to understand why he used this name. Later the Spaniards dropped this uncomplimentary word and renamed them the Marianas in honor of Maria Anna, the widow of King Philip IV of Spain.

The natives who first settled on Guam had called that island Iubagana. The Spaniards later shortened that to Guan. Now it's called Guam.

THREE WARS

From 1696 on the Marianas belonged to Spain. Then in 1898 the Spanish-American War broke out. The American cruiser *Charleston* sailed into the harbor of Apra on the island of Guam and bombarded the Spanish fort there. But the Spanish governor had not even heard of any war. He thought the Americans were firing a salute in his honor. So he sent a note of apology to the American commander, saying he was sorry he could not return the salute, for he was all out of gunpowder. Needless to say he had to surrender. When the war ended Guam was ceded to the United States by Spain. But the other islands remained Spanish until they were sold to Germany.

Then came the First World War. After the German defeat these German islands were turned over to Japan to ad-

minister for the League of Nations. The arrangement was called a mandate.

Finally the Second World War broke out. Japan attacked Pearl Harbor on December 7, 1941. Two days later Guam fell to them. Then for almost four years the Japanese held the island. But the Americans came back on July 20, 1944, and after some terrible fighting during which the island was blown to fragments the Japanese were compelled to surrender.

THE PRESENT GOVERNMENT

Guam is now an Unincorporated Territory of the United States. It is administered by the Department of the Interior. The people are American citizens, but they have no right to vote in national elections, and they are not represented in Congress. Nevertheless the United States has spent hundreds of millions of dollars in rebuilding the island and improving the lot of the people. The capital is Agaña.

WHAT THE ISLAND IS LIKE

Guam is 5,100 miles west of San Francisco and 3,340 miles west of Honolulu. It's a small island, 30 miles long and from 4 to 10 wide. It has a total population now of about 73,000 people. About 36,000 are Guamanians, 25,000 are Americans stationed on the island, and about 12,000 are Filipinos brought in under contract as laborers.

Guam is the most southerly of the Marianas. The most northerly is the island of Maug. This word is "Guam" spelled backwards, but this is only accidental.

Guam has volcanic hills in the south, a limestone plateau in the north.

THE CHAMORROS

The first settlers came from the Philippines. They called themselves Chamorros. The tongue they spoke was not a

Micronesian dialect. It was a distinct language. In this language the name *Chamorri* means "chief." The language is spoken everywhere in the homes of the people, but a great deal of Spanish is now mixed up with it.

THE ECONOMY OF THE ISLANDS

The people live mostly in villages, which they leave each morning to work their farms. The most important crop is corn. Each farm has an acre or two for this crop, about the same amount for bananas, breadfruit, papayas, melons, pineapples, cassava, sweet potatoes, rice, sugar cane, cotton, coffee, and cocoa. There are a few scrawny cattle, and almost every farmer has a carabao, so that another third of the land is usually reserved for pasturage. The chief exports are copra and mother-of-pearl.

TYPHOONS

Guam is in the typhoon area. The worst tropical storm ever known there, the typhoon Karen, ripped through the island in the middle of November 1962, injuring hundreds of people and doing hundreds of millions of dollars worth of damage. The winds rose to 172 miles an hour, four out of five houses lost their roofs, about half the people were left homeless. The governor reported that this terrible storm was worse than the 1944 shelling, when the United States troops invaded the island to liberate it from the Japanese.

Lourdes Quidachay Untalan is a Guamanian girl who knows what typhoons are. Her father is a carpenter and she wants to be a nurse. John San Agustin Fernandez goes to a well-known Catholic school. His father is a plumber.

MY SCHOOL IS IN QUONSET HUTS

by Lourdes Quidachay Untalan

GUAM WAS BLOWN TO PIECES DURING THE WAR

The island of Guam was captured by the Japanese at the beginning of the Second World War, but finally the Japanese were driven out again by the Americans. There wasn't very much left of the capital, Agaña, after all the bombings. It was just blown to pieces. And one of the very first things the Americans did, when they came back, was to push the ruins of many of the buildings into the sea with great bulldozers. They actually made some new land that way.

Even now, while there are a number of fine new buildings, there are many open spaces, many lots covered with weeds and brush, where there used to be buildings. There are many temporary buildings too. The George Washington High School, where I go, meets in huge quonset huts, which, as you know, are semi-circular buildings made of corrugated iron. They were used during the war for all kinds of military purposes and they make very good school buildings. We occupy about thirty of them. Some are undivided and are used for gymnasium, study hall, and such things. Others are divided into classrooms. The huts we use are very big. They must be about two hundred feet long.

In Agaña these huts are used for many other purposes also. The officers use them for their houses. They are used for public buildings. They are used everywhere for stores, sometimes with a false front, so that you don't know it is a quonset until you are inside.

MY HOUSE IN AGAÑA

My name is Lourdes Quidachay Untalan, and I was born in Mongmong Village, which is a part of Agaña, sixteen years ago. I still live in the same village and even in the same house. It is a wooden house of one story with a shingle roof. There are only two rooms in it. One of them is the kitchen, and the other room is where we all sleep. This second room is pretty large, about twenty by twenty-three feet. It is sheathed inside with wood and divided by curtains. Besides my father and mother there are nine children, and we all have beds to sleep on, except for the baby who sleeps with my mother, the next two older boys who sleep with my grandmother next door, and two others who sleep on mats laid on the floor. We have a kerosene stove, an electric refrigerator, and running water. We have a table and chairs in the kitchen and all the family gets together for meals there. The toilet is outside.

There are about six hundred people living in Mongmong Village. Many of these are farmers, and some of them work on lands in other places. Other people work for the United States Navy here, and still others for the territorial government.

MY FATHER IS A CARPENTER

My father is Jesus Reyes Untalan. He was born in the same village, and is a carpenter, working for my uncle. During the Japanese occupation of the island he had to work for them, but they treated him all right.

My mother's name is Carmen Quidachay Untalan. She was

born in Mongmong Village also, and was married when she was seventeen.

The oldest of the children is Rosa. She is seventeen and is a junior in my high school. She wants to become a Wave or an airplane hostess. Then I come, and after me is Asunción, who is fourteen. She is in the eighth grade of elementary school and wants to be a hostess. Julita is twelve. She is in the sixth grade. Joseph, who is ten, and Teresita, who is nine, are both in the fourth grade. Pedro is eight and in the second grade. Antonio is five and too young for school, and the baby Maria is a year old.

I was something of a tomboy when I was small. I loved to climb trees and build houses in the woods out of branches.

MY THREE SCHOOLS

When I was six I went to primary school not far from home and I was there for four years. Then for another four years I went to the elementary school which was a little less than a mile from my house. Now I am a freshman in George Washington High School, which was established after the war.

I am taking art, general science, civics, mathematics, English, and gym. I like my English best, and I want to go to the States and study nursing, perhaps to become a doctor. This will probably be in California. I should like to practice nursing in the States for a couple of years, and then take a trip around the world before coming back to Guam. This, at least, is my ambition. The family can help me with my training, but I am hoping to get a scholarship.

MY SCHEDULE

I get up at six thirty and prepare lunches for Julita, Joseph, Teresita, and Pedro, mostly sandwiches. At seven I have breakfast: bread with butter, cheese, peanut butter, or jam, with a glass of milk. I leave at seven thirty for school. School doesn't begin until eight, and I like to talk with my friends beforehand. There are three class periods from eight to eleven twenty and then it's time for lunch. Some of the girls play volleyball during the lunch period, but I don't, for I have to go home. We eat the lunch I prepared in the morning. My mother is not well, and so the children do most of the work. For lunch we have soup, rice, meat, and some cold drink like a coke or orange juice. We don't have any dessert.

School begins again at twelve fifteen and lasts until three thirty. There are three more periods. Then I go home, clean the house, and help with the washing and ironing. The four older girls wash the baby's diapers. Twice a week I wash my father's and mother's clothes along with my own. After these chores are done I cook the dinner, which is much like our lunch. Dinner is at seven. We have different kinds of food but I like barbecued chicken best.

I usually have about an hour and a half of homework and I go to bed at nine.

OUTSIDE SCHOOL

Saturdays I have a good deal of work to do around the house in the morning. After lunch I usually take a nap and then go to see some other girls. We play records. At home we have a radio but no television. My grandmother next door does have a television set, however, and sometimes I go over to watch it. I often have a little homework to do. I seldom go to the movies, but I play checkers with the other girls in the family. We have rabbits but I don't have to take care of them.

On Sundays I go to the six-o'clock Mass, getting up at five. The Mass is at the Mongmong church. I am home for breakfast at seven. The rest of the morning I play records or go to my grandmother's to watch television. The family has a Dodge car, and sometimes we go for a drive somewhere around the island. But I have never been off the island at all.

We have a Christmas vacation from December 24 to January 2, a few days at Easter, and a long vacation from June 3 to August 1. I can swim a little but I seldom go to the beach.

We always have a carnival for five days ending July 21. Then every village chooses a queen and from all these queens the Queen of Guam is chosen at Agaña.

Every village has a saint's day also.

I speak English and Guamanian. We always talk Guamanian at home. Guamanian is a mixture of the old Chamorro tongue and Spanish. For instance, we say *Hafa dai* for "hello." This is Chamorro. But we say *adios* for "good-by." This is Spanish.

Guam is in the area of the typhoons. In 1950 our house was shaking so badly we thought it was going to blow away, but we managed to get out of it. In 1958 the typhoon Lola was terrible. The typhoon did a lot of damage, but we did not have to leave our home.

MY SCHOOL WAS NAMED FOR A GUAMANIAN HERO

by John San Agustin Fernandez

FATHER DUENAS

My school is the Father Duenas Memorial School. Father Duenas was a Catholic priest who was killed by the Japanese during the occupation because he resisted them. He is not considered a martyr by the church, since he was killed not because of his faith but because of his patriotism. But he has become a hero in the history of our territory.

Until recently this school, which has a fine group of new buildings, was operated by the Stigmatine Fathers. Now the Capuchins have taken it over.

WE HAVE TWO HOUSES

I was born sixteen years ago in Agaña, and I lived there for about a year before we moved to Dededo Village, which is about six or seven miles north of Agaña. The house we now live in is a wooden house with four bedrooms, a kitchen, a dining room, and an inside toilet. The roof is of corrugated iron.

We have another house at Tamuning about five miles away. It is made of cement blocks with a corrugated iron roof and has three bedrooms. We rent this house when we can, and when we can't we sometimes live in it. Both of our houses have modern furniture, electric lights, running water, electric stoves, and refrigerators.

MY FAMILY

My father's name is José Lujan Fernandez. He is a plumber working for the government. He is half Spanish and was born on the island.

My mother has some Filipino blood. Her name is Ana San Agustin Fernandez, and she was born on the island also.

I have three brothers and four sisters. They come in this order. First is Rita who is thirty years old, married, with two children. Then comes Jesus who is twenty-eight, married, with ten children. Francisco is also twenty-eight, married, with three children. Maria is twenty-seven, married, with three children. Anita is twenty-five. She is married but has no children. Lourdes is twenty-four and single. She works as a secretary. José is twenty-three, unmarried and working as a boilerman, third class, on a U.S. aircraft carrier. He has studied for the anti-submarine service. I am the youngest in the family.

CATHOLIC SCHOOLS

I first went to school in a Catholic kindergarten when I was five. It was near my home and I was there for one year. Then for four years I went to a Catholic primary school, and then to an elementary school in the same building. At fourteen I came to Father Duenas Memorial School. This is now my second year here. I am in the tenth grade.

My studies are Latin, English, geometry, biology, religion, and speech. I like my geometry and biology best. I want to go on from here to college.

SCHOOL LIFE

At six thirty I get up and have my breakfast of eggs, bacon, bread and butter, and milk. Sometimes I have fruit juice too. At seven thirty I start for school. Sometimes I go in a bus, and sometimes my father drives me in his 1959 Edsel.

School begins at eight thirty and lasts until eleven forty-five. There are four forty-five-minute periods. Our lunch period lasts until twelve thirty. I buy my lunch at the school cafeteria and it costs thirty-five cents. We usually have soup, spaghetti, bread and butter, salad, sometimes a dessert, and milk. Often we have meat and vegetables.

From twelve thirty to three there are afternoon classes and then usually the car comes for me.

I play football, baseball, and basketball at the school.

We have supper about six, chicken or steak, vegetables, sometimes salad, ice cream or fruit. My homework takes about two hours. Then I often watch television. I am usually in bed by nine or nine thirty. Sometimes I play cards in the evening. I have about five pigeons and sixty hens. That means we have plenty of eggs for ourselves and some to give away to our friends.

HUNTING AND FISHING

On Saturday I play games. Sometimes I take my .22 caliber rifle and go shooting. I get small birds and some quail. We don't eat the small birds, but the quail and the wild pigeons I sometimes get are very good eating. Sometimes I go fishing around the reefs that encircle the island. I use a spear gun to fish with. On Saturdays I work around the house also, cutting the lawn and such things. Sometimes we go for a drive about the island, but I have never been away from Guam. In the evening I often watch TV.

MASS AND RELIGIOUS FIESTAS

I go to Mass in the Dededo Church at seven thirty on Sunday and then come home for breakfast. The rest of the day is like any Saturday, though sometimes I may spend a lot of time reading at home.

At Christmas we have a spruce tree that is imported from the States. We erect it in the house and have presents either on Christmas eve or on Christmas morning.

Santa Barbara is the patron saint of my parish, and her fiesta takes place the first Saturday and Sunday of December. We always have a religious procession, but we have lots of fun with merry-go-rounds and things like that.

VACATIONS

The long vacation is from early June to the end of August. When the other house is not rented we go there. That house is nearer the beach. Next summer I may try to make some money during vacation by working at a service station or by mowing lawns.

10. OKINAWA

THE ROPE IN THE SEA

THE RIM OF ASIA

There is a long line of islands just off the Asiatic mainland that reaches from Alaska to Taiwan. The Aleutians stretch from Alaska to Kamchatka. Then the Kuriles extend to Japan. South of Japan are the Ryukyus, 775 miles of little islands that separate the East China Sea to the west from the Philippine Sea to the east. The giant of our childhood fairy tales could have walked all the way on these steppingstones from our forty-ninth state to Taiwan without wetting his feet.

People call them the Rim of Asia.

THE FLOATING DRAGON

The Ryukyus are the islands of this chain that we are now interested in. The name originally meant the "Floating Dragon." Later one of the Ming emperors changed the Chinese characters so that they would mean "Precious Beads." One writer says that they are "like an earthworm that has been chopped to bits." The main islands are really the peaks of an old mountain chain, but the smaller islands are often flat and of coral formation.

A quarter of these islands is not inhabited, but those that have people are thickly populated. Altogether there are 1,850 square miles of land with more than a million people living on them. That's about 1,300 persons to every square mile. The United States has only 50 to each square mile.

THE ROPE IN THE SEA

The Ryukyu Archipelago is divided into four major island groups with over a hundred islands in them. There are, however, numberless rocks and reefs everywhere.

The largest of the Ryukyus is called Okinawa, and the name means "Rope in the Sea." Most of us had never heard of Okinawa before the Second World War, but we've heard a great deal about it since that time. It lies just about halfway between Tokyo in Japan and Manila in the Philippines. It's sixty-five miles long and from two to twelve miles wide. It has a population of about 650,000. Naha is the chief city. There are low mountains and rolling hills on Okinawa. Around the island are coral reefs.

THREE STREAMS OF PEOPLE

The first stream of people who came to Okinawa were related to the Ainus in northern Japan. They were a small, hairy people who seem to have come down from Siberia through the Japanese islands and the northern Ryukyus. They were not like the Japanese or the Chinese. They were more like the people of Europe, and their language was not related to any other known speech in the world.

Then came the people who wandered up from Indonesia through the Philippines and Taiwan. They were Malayans.

Lastly appeared the Manchurians and Mongolians who came through Korea and Japan.

A TANGLED HISTORY

The early history of Okinawa is a confused tale. There were kings there in the beginning, but China and Japan vied with each other to control them. Foreign nations also appeared on the scene. French, British, and Dutch plotted for power. Our own Admiral Matthew Perry landed in Okinawa on May 26, 1853, before he sailed for Japan. His men called him "Old Matt," and he came in American war vessels which had never been seen before in the East. They not only had sails, they had also engines and paddle wheels and smokestacks. The people in Japan called them the "evil-looking black ships," because they belched forth black smoke. Perry thought Okinawa could become an important center for American trade, but his plan was never carried out.

Japan made the Ryukyus a province in 1879. Then in 1945 the Second World War hit the island. This was the last of the great Pacific campaigns. It began on Easter Sunday and lasted for three months. It was a very bloody struggle. The United States had 48,000 casualties, 12,000 of them killed. The Japanese lost 103,000 of their 120,000 men. One hundred forty thousand civilians died. More than nine-tenths of all the buildings were destroyed.

THE *KAMIKAZE*

In Japanese this word means "the divine wind." It was the name the people gave to the typhoon that destroyed the fleet of the mighty Mongol emperor, Kublai Khan, on his way to invade Japan in 1281. During the Second World War the Japanese gave the name to a suicide air force. The flyers deliberately crashed their bomb-laden planes on the decks of American warships. The American navy suffered severe losses because of them at Okinawa.

HARA-KIRI

Still the Japanese were defeated. On June 23, 1945, the two Japanese generals came out of the mouth of the cave which was their headquarters, spread a white cloth on the ground, sat down on it, and plunged their swords into their bowels. This was what the Japanese called "hara-kiri." Since the generals had lost the battle, they considered it their last duty to their emperor to commit hara-kiri.

THE VIRGINS' CAVE

Another sad tale has to do with the Virgins' Cave. There were many caves in Okinawa and they had been used by the Japanese soldiers. In the mopping-up operation at the end of the conflict the American soldiers had to clean out these caves. At the mouth of one of them they called out several times to the occupants to surrender, but there was no reply. So they threw their bombs and directed their flame-throwers into the interior. After it was over they found that the cave was filled with 120 high school girls, a nurses' corps that had been using the cave as a hospital. Only three girls and one teacher survived.

AFTER THE PEACE

The peace treaty in September, 1951, gave the United States a temporary trusteeship over all the Ryukyus south of the twenty-ninth parallel north. Two years later we returned many of these islands to Japan. But even before the peace treaty we had replaced the military government by the USCAR (the United States Civil Administration of the Ryukyus).

In these recent years the United States has spent billions of dollars in strengthening Okinawa and making it our front line of defense in the Pacific. The Korean War showed us how vital Okinawa was to us. It's only 350 miles from Red China. Today it's the "Keystone of the Pacific."

ECONOMIC PROSPECTS

These are not bright. The islanders do not begin to produce as much rice as they eat. There are only about 275 acres of soil for farming and this soil is thin. The people raise sugar and export it to Japan, where their partially refined "black sugar" is liked. They also send many millions of silkworm eggs to Japan. The mulberry trees on which the worms feed grow all the year round in Okinawa, but only for six months of the year in Japan. The Okinawans have crossed Chinese- and Japanese-type moths to get a stronger and longer thread.

There are pearl farms in Okinawa also, where fine cultured black pearls (they are really a smoky gray in color) are produced.

Textiles are manufactured. *Jofu* is made from ramie fiber. The ancient Egyptians wrapped their mummies in this cloth. It is seven times as strong as silk, and it's light, cool, and beautiful. *Bashofu* is another thin, crisp textile, made from the male banana plant. Okinawa is the only place in the world where this cloth is made. There is a big demand for these two fabrics.

There are very fragrant lilies growing in Okinawa and great quantities of them are exported.

But the chief export of all is people. Many of the Okinawans leave their crowded homeland for Japan, South America, and the United States.

JAPANESE CUSTOMS

Japanese influence is very strong in Okinawa. Japanese has been taught in the schools for sixty years and more, and most of the people feel that they are Japanese and want Okinawa turned back to Japan. Many of their houses are Japanese in character, they wear kimonos at home, and often carry fans. Their religion has come mostly through Japan, their ceremonies, customs, and festivals are mainly Japanese.

JAPANESE FESTIVALS

The August Moon Festival is one of the loveliest of the whole year. The people gather on hilltops or in their homes with doors open to the full moon. There is much music on the drums and samisens and much dancing and feasting.

The Japanese bullfight is very different from the Spanish bullfight. There are no matadors. Two specially trained Brahman bulls fight each other. The bulls pound and butt each other until one or the other of them turns tail and flees. The fight lasts for ten to thirty minutes.

At the village of Nago the porpoises come in from the sea during February. Then the fishermen in their canoes try to surround them and drive them in to the shore where they can be killed.

Kinjo Ikuku is a girl who lives in Naha City. She says she doesn't belong to any church. Heshiki Tetsuo is a boy who lives in a little farming village on the southeast side of Okinawa. He says he is a Christian. Both of these young people tell us of other customs and festivals and of their life on the island.

I LIVE IN TYPHOON ALLEY

by Kinjo Ikuku

I KNOW WHAT TYPHOONS ARE

I am a girl and I don't know why typhoons are always named for girls in my country, but they always are. Recently we have had two typhoons, called Emma and Freda. They were not very bad, however. Freda brought what the boys called good "kite-flying winds," but some of our typhoons have been terrible. They are usually born just east of the Philippines, and then they often travel to the north through what we call Typhoon alley over Taiwan and the Ryukyu Islands to Japan.

WHERE I LIVE

I live in Naha City, which is the capital of Okinawa in the Ryukyu Islands, so I know what typhoons are. I don't like them.

My first name is Ikuku, but my family often calls me Ikuchan. *Chan* means "lovely," but it's just an affectionate nickname in my family. I was born in Naha City sixteen years ago. I have lived in my present house for seven years. The sides of the house are of corrugated iron and the roof is of tiles. Inside it is a real Japanese house. There are sliding doors and windows. When we come in we take off our shoes and step up on a little platform where we put on slippers. We do this so we shall not bring dirt into the house, and so we shall not hurt the "straw mats," called *tatami*, which are laid on the floor. Most Japanese houses have a "little alcove" in the living room, called a *tokonomo*. Usually there is a lovely picture hanging there and a vase of flowers. But in our house we have no tokonomo.

We have three rooms and a separate kitchen. We cook on an oil stove in the kitchen, but to keep warm in the winter we use a *hibachi*, which is a low brazier where we burn charcoal.

THE FAMILY

My father's name is Kikuzo. He makes soy sauce and sells it all on the island. The Japanese people use a great deal of this sauce. My father was born in Naha City, and during the war he was in the Japanese army. He loves us children very much and is doing everything he can to help us get along.

Mother's name is Chiyo. She was born in Naha City and weaves cotton cloth, which she sells to the stores. The oldest child is a girl of thirty, named Toyoko. She is married and has five children. Her husband is a policeman. Next comes a boy of twenty-eight, named Katsuharu. He is married and has four children. He runs a grocery shop. Then I come and after me is a boy of thirteen, who is in the sixth year of the primary school. His name is Kiyoshi and he wants to be a jet pilot.

During the war my father sent the older children to Japan, where he thought they would be safer. They went to Miako, which is a city on the big southern island of Kyushu. They went by boat and were there about a year. They played with the Japanese children there, and used to love picking the wild flowers. When they came back after the year they found that our house in Okinawa had been destroyed. For a time the family lived in my uncle's house.

SCHOOL AT SEVEN

I first went to school when I was seven. This was a kindergarten and I was there for one year. Then I went to primary school for six years. Now I am in the third grade of junior high. Next March I will graduate. Then if I pass the examinations I will enter high school. But only about one out of two students pass.

I have nine subjects in school: English, mathematics, social studies, general science, physical education, music, drawing, art, and home economics. I like my general science best of all and I am much interested in anatomy. Later, if it is possible, I should like to study medicine. My father is trying to save some money to send me to medical school in Tokyo. But if I ever become a doctor I should like to come back to the Ryukyu Islands to practice.

In my school the boys wear a black uniform with silver-like buttons, and a cap with a band of white tape around it. But the girls do not have uniforms. I'm sorry about that for I'd like to have a uniform.

I am always up at six o'clock in the morning. I have my breakfast at seven ten, rice, seaweed, and soy sauce. I eat fish on the rice too, and I have tea to drink. It takes me from fifteen to twenty minutes to walk to school and school lasts from nine to three thirty. At one I eat my lunch, which I have brought from home, rice and eggs, fish, chicken, or meat. I have nothing to drink with my lunch.

When I go home at three thirty I help my mother with the housework, cleaning, cooking, making beds. I have about an hour's homework to do. Sometimes I go to the movies, either in the afternoon or the evening. If I have time I may visit my friends.

I have dinner at seven thirty and this is the big meal of the day, meat, chicken, or fish with rice. We never have any dessert and we don't eat much fruit. We have tea to drink.

On Saturday we have school just as we do on every other day. That is because I am going to take the examinations. Those who don't have to take them only go in the morning.

I WORSHIP MY ANCESTORS

I don't belong to any church, either Christian or Japanese, and so I don't go to a service on Sunday. Twice a year I go to the cemetery to worship my ancestors. Sunday is usually a free day for me. I spend most of the time at home. I play cards, and a Japanese game which is called *Shogi*. It is something like checkers, but not quite the same. I have one special friend who is in school with me. We live far apart so I seldom see her except in school.

Many of the hillsides in Okinawa are covered with tombs made of concrete. They are called turtle-back tombs, and the top of them is shaped just like a turtle's back. Once a year there comes the *O-bon* festival, or "the feast of the dead." This falls in the sixth month of the lunar year, and it is believed that then the spirits of the dead come back to meet with the living people. We burn incense to welcome the spirits and we have a big meal at the altar, on which food is set out for the returning spirits. There is a great feast on the third day with dances and entertainment. When the spirits see how happy we all are they go back to heaven for another year. Each of the spirits receives two stalks of sugar cane to be used as walking sticks on the way back to their dark world.

It used to be the custom to open the tomb two or three

years after death, when young, unmarried girls like me had to scrape and wash the bones. Then the bones were put into jars. This custom is not so common now as it used to be, I'm very glad to say.

HAPPY NEW YEAR

The O-bon festival at the end is very gay, but the New Year's festival is much more fun. It is the happiest of all the holidays. In front of each gate are placed a bamboo and a pine tree. A straw rope is stretched across the gate. Offerings are made to our ancestors. The boys and girls go round to the different houses and get candy, fruit, cakes, and money. Everything starts fresh on New Year's. We pay everything we owe, we have new kimonos, and *geta,* which are "wooden shoes," and we go to the temple to pray for health and prosperity.

The festival lasts for three days. The girls play games. The boys spin tops and fly kites.

I can speak Japanese and Okinawan. Before the war many people had no chance to study Japanese and could not speak it. But they all spoke Okinawan. Now most people speak Japanese and English. English is compulsory from the first year in junior high.

THE OKINAWAN LANGUAGE

Okinawan is very different from Japanese, but there are many Japanese words in it. The Japanese for "thank you very much" is *arigato gozaimasu.* In Okinawan we say *nihe debiru.* On the other hand, in both languages we say *sayonara* for "good-by." Some common English words are spoken and understood by everybody: *hello, bye-bye, okay, thank you.*

I have traveled everywhere over my island, but nowhere else except to Japan.

I LIVE IN AN OKINAWAN VILLAGE

by Heshiki Tetsuo

OKINAWAN FESTIVALS

Of all the holidays in the year I think I like Christmas best because we have a winter vacation then. This year we're going to have presents for the first time. Giving presents hasn't been a custom for us in Okinawa.

During the harvest festival we have a tug of war between our village and another village, which is lots of fun. The rice straw, which has just been cut, is braided to make a huge rope. Sometimes it's one thousand feet long, and often it's from three to five feet in diameter. One rope is made for each village, and they are then carried through the streets to the beach. There they are fastened together, and as soon as they are connected the men, women, and children grab a lot of small straw ropes that are tied to the big one and the tug of war begins. This comes in the ninth month of the lunar year.

The fifth month of the lunar year the fishing villages along the coast of Okinawa have dragon-boat races and I always go to see them. The boats are painted in bright colors to represent dragons. One man in each boat beats a drum and the boats have to race out to a marker and then return.

MY VILLAGE

My village is on the southeast side of Okinawa and is called Nishi Hara-Son. It's within sight of the place where Lieutenant General Simon Bolivar Buckner, Jr., the American commander in the battle of Okinawa, was killed a few days before the Japanese surrendered. It is also near the place called Suicide Cliff, where the general commanding the Japanese army and his chief of staff killed themselves.

My village is not far from the shore, but it isn't a fishing village. It's a farming village. There are about 150 people in it. They grow sugar cane mostly, but also sweet potatoes and other vegetables. There is a factory for making brown sugar, though we call it black sugar. There is a theater in the village, a few shops, a Christian Sunday School, but no church or temple.

MY PARENTS AND THE CHILDREN

My father is Shizuo. He is employed in the office of the superintendent of schools. He is in charge of social welfare. He used to be a teacher and was in the Japanese army before the Second World War, but he did not fight in this war.

My mother's name is Ritsoko. She is a teacher of the sixth grade in the Nishi Hara-Son Elementary School. She was born in Koza City, which is in the center of Okinawa.

There are four boys and two girls in my family. Yoshikiro is eighteen. He has finished school and is now at home. He hasn't yet found a job. My name is Tetsuo and I come next. I am sixteen. Then comes my brother Tsunehiro, who is thirteen and in the sixth grade of the primary school. Katsuya is a boy of ten and is in the fourth grade. My sister Chieko is eight and is in the first grade. Last comes my sister Reiko who is four and not yet in school.

My grandmother lives with us too. She is sixty years old.

A JAPANESE HOUSE

We have always lived in the same house ever since I was born. It's a wooden, unpainted house. The Japanese seldom use paint on their houses either inside or out. There are cement tiles on the roof. Many of the Okinawan houses have little porcelain lions on the roof. The lion is a strong animal and people think that the lion on the roof protects them from harm. Our house, however, doesn't have one. All our windows are double. The outside ones are of glass, the inside ones of paper. The doors slide, and when you come in through the front entrance you have to pass through three doors. The outside one is wooden, the next is glass, and the inside one is paper. There are four rooms in the house besides the kitchen. We use a *hibachi* to keep warm in the winter and we boil water on it for our tea. In the living room we have a *tokonomo* and hanging in it is a scroll with Japanese handwriting on it. Our floors are covered with *tatami* mats and we sleep on mattresses that are spread on the floor with quilts and blankets.

MY LIFE AT SCHOOL

I went to kindergarten for one year when I was six, and then for six years more I was in primary school. Now I am in the third year of the junior high school. I am studying Japanese literature, mathematics, social science, English, general science, physical education, music, art, and agricultural science. Instead of agricultural science the girls take home economics. I like mathematics and English best of all. I have been studying English for three years. I should like to be a teacher.

My day begins at seven o'clock and I have breakfast at seven thirty, rice, eggs, soup, and tea. I live just behind the school. School lasts from nine until three thirty-five. I bring my lunch from home and eat it at twelve fifty. It's usually rice with meat or fish or fried prawns, and vegetables. After lunch I play for a while in the school yard. I play baseball, volleyball, and track. I am on the school basketball team, and play with other teams in a school league.

I am preparing for my high school examination, and so I have an extra hour and a half of study after other students go home. I have an hour's homework to do also either before or after dinner. For dinner I have soup, fried rice, and meat. In the winter we have dishes like *sukiyaki,* which consists of meat, bean curds, and vegetables with a delicious sauce.

After dinner I may read or play games like chess or shogi. The latter looks like checkers but it isn't. We have a maid in the house, since both father and mother work, but I always make my own bed. I am usually asleep by eleven or twelve.

All the boys and girls go to school on Saturday mornings, but I go also in the afternoons, because I am going to take the high school examinations.

I AM A CHRISTIAN

I go to the village Sunday School on Sunday morning. In the afternoon I sometimes go to Naha City to watch a volleyball or basketball game. I have no homework to do on Sundays.

My father and mother have no religion, but three times a year they go to the cemetery to bring flowers to the family tombs.

THE LONG VACATION

Our long vacation in the summer lasts from July 25 to the end of August. I play a good deal of basketball then, and I take Red Cross instruction. We have classes in swimming and first-aid. Often I go on picnics to different places on the island. I have traveled almost everywhere on Okinawa but I have never been off the island.

I speak Japanese, Okinawan, and a little English.

十村